THE CADILLAC STORY

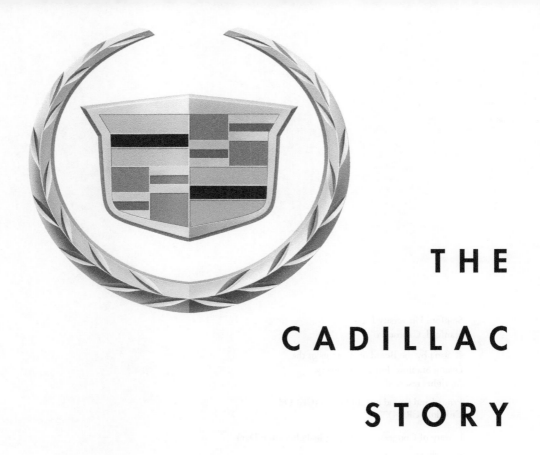

THE
CADILLAC
STORY

The Postwar Years

Thomas E. Bonsall

STANFORD GENERAL BOOKS
An Imprint of Stanford University Press
Stanford, California 2004

Stanford University Press
Stanford, California

© 2004 by the Board of Trustees of the
Leland Stanford Junior University.
All rights reserved.

Printed and bound by CPI Group (UK) Ltd,
Croydon, CR0 4YY

Library of Congress Cataloging-in-Publication Data

Bonsall, Thomas E.
    The Cadillac story : the postwar years / Thomas E. Bonsall.
        p.   cm.
    Includes bibliographical references and index.
    ISBN 0-8047-4942-6 (alk. paper)
        1. Cadillac automobile—History.   2. General Motors Corporation—
Cadillac Motor Car Division—History.   I. Title.
TL215.C27 B65   2003
629.222'09—dc22   2003015377

Original Printing 2003

Last figure below indicates year of this printing:
12   11   10   09   08   07   06   05   04   03

Designed by James P. Brommer
Typeset in 11/15 Garamond

Contents

Contents

Acknowledgments

The author is indebted to numerous individuals and organizations who have assisted the research that went into this book. This list includes the late Norb Bartos, who was a member of Cadillac's public relations staff for nearly forty years, and unfailingly supported my historical research into the marque. Richard Stout, a former member of the product planning staff at the General Motors then Lincoln-Mercury Division then Packard and still later back at Lincoln-Mercury Division again, submitted to several invaluable interviews. Few understood the dynamics of the industry better than Dick Stout did. Bob Stempel, Strother MacMinn, Frank Hershey, John Grettenberger and William Hoglund each gave several interviews over the years, and this book would be very different without their cooperation. Numerous people within General Motors assisted in ways large and small through the years from various departments, including Cadillac Motor Car Division, the Design Staff, and GM Photographic.

Acknowledgments

THE CADILLAC STORY

1936 Series Sixty coupe.

Introduction

CADILLAC CELEBRATED its 100th Anniversary in 2002. Very few brands have achieved that milestone, so there must have been something significant going on. And, indeed, the Cadillac story is more than the story of a car company. It is, in many ways, the story of the American automobile industry itself, which is to say, one of the most important dramas in modern American history. The automobile industry has, as much as any industry, driven America's growth in the 20th Century and defined who we are as a people: mobile and prosperous. Cadillac, again and again, played a critical role in that story.

In the years prior to World War I, Cadillac introduced so many developments of historic impact that it, to an amazing degree, defined the automobile as we have come to know it. In addition, were it not for Cadillac, General Motors would probably not exist today. Perhaps of even greater importance, Cadillac led the drive for quality manufacturing techniques that revolutionized industry around the world and without which modern mass production would have been an impossibility. In the 1920s, Cadillac was the first car company to seek the services of a professional design staff, and the success of that effort transformed the way in which cars were conceived and developed throughout the industry. In the depths of the Great Depression, Cadillac redefined itself and the luxury market. After World War II, Cadillac epitomized the expansive prosperity of America. Then, in the 1980s, Cadillac epitomized the industrial crisis that had suddenly overtaken us. Today, Cadillac's struggle to survive in a furiously competitive—and suddenly international—automobile industry mirrors the challenges facing American industry, as a whole. And, Cadillac's success in meeting those challenges will have much to say about the future of American industry, in general, and of General Motors, in particular.

The Cadillac story is the stuff of great novels. It is filled with drama and intrigue. It includes exciting triumphs and bitter failures. Some of the most fascinating people in the history of America in the 20th Century appear upon its pages. And, like most great stories, it is littered with ironies and coincidences. In fact, the story began with a chance encounter between two of the most important men in the history of the automobile—the two Henrys, Leland and Ford.

Henry Martyn Leland remains one of the unsung heroes of the early American auto industry. He was already nationally renowned as the founder of the machine tool-making firm of Leland and Faulconer when he took on supervisory responsibilities for the Henry Ford Company in 1902—an action prompted by Ford's investors that immediately infuriated Ford.

The Henry Ford involved was not the internationally famous Henry Ford of legend, but the gifted mechanic-with-a-dream in the years that predated his success and fame. That dream was to build automobiles, and his Odyssey led him eventually, through a curious combination of circumstances, to Henry Martyn Leland. Leland was a sober-minded craftsman who, by all accounts, had given the automobile little thought. Yet, the results—direct and indirect —of their encounter would set in motion a train of events that ultimately led to the creation of no less than three of the greatest names in American motoring: Cadillac, Ford, and Lincoln.

Then as later, Henry Ford didn't like anyone trying to tell him what to do. Following Ford's angry departure—to ultimately found the Ford Motor Company—the frantic investors in the enterprise implored Leland and his son, Wilfred, to take a major role in the firm. Although at first reluctant, Leland finally agreed to do so. And, since Ford's termination agreement had denied them the use of the Ford name, another had to be found. In due course, they decided to rename the company in honor of the founder of Detroit and, in this way, the Cadillac Automobile Company was born.

Almost immediately upon assuming a key role at Cadillac, Leland began to earn an international reputation for the extraordinary quality of his products. Most notably, under his direction Cadillac was the first auto maker to use fully interchangeable parts. This was a true watershed development without which the modern mass production techniques (pioneered, ironically, by Henry Ford) would have been an impossibility, and whose impact extended far beyond the confines of the auto industry.

Curiously, though, Leland had no official capacity at Cadillac for several years after the departure of Henry Ford. Leland supplied most of the engines and chassis components through Leland and Faulconer. Cadillac's president, Lemmuel Bowen, was a big Leland supporter and even saw to it that Leland was elected to the board of directors and given some stock. Cadillac production remained steady at around 2,400 cars during 1904, which made Cadillac one of the largest auto producers in the nation.

Eventually, Leland and Faulconer merged with Cadillac and the Cadillac Motor Car Company came into being. A few years after that, Cadillac was acquired by General Motors. Henry Leland stuck around for a few years, then had a falling out with William C. Durant who ran GM and left to start another car company: Lincoln. That effort quickly faltered due to a sudden, sharp recession in the nation's economy, but Ford Motor Company rode to the rescue. This set the stage for the head-to-head battle that has raged for more than eighty years between the two luxury brands. Initially, too, there were other contenders. Packard and Pierce-Arrow were major competitors in the luxury field in the years leading up to the Great Depression. In fact, Packard led the field until it faltered in the mid-1930s. At least it survived into the postwar period, unlike Pierce-Arrow, which succumbed in 1938.

After the end of World War II, though, it was really a two-brand fight between Cadillac and Lincoln—with Cadillac generally well in the lead. The key to this was the autonomous divisional structure developed at GM by Alfred Sloan, president and then chairman for nearly forty years. The basic idea was to run the individual divisions insofar as possible as independent automobile manufacturers, each with its own design, engineering, manufacturing, and marketing departments. What this approach permitted at Cadillac was remarkable fidelity to the basic concept of what a Cadillac was. Cadillacs might change dramatically in engineering or appearance from one year to the next, but they always retained Cadillac styling cues that made them seem the same.

In contrast, Lincoln in the postwar era was essentially little more than a sales and marketing department within Ford Motor Company. Since it did not control the product, it was powerless to enforce a given Lincoln concept. Each of the early postwar cars, for example, were victims of this lack of focus. The 1949–51, 1952–55, 1956–57, 1958–60, and 1961–65 series cars were so lacking in continuity they could have been built by five different car companies.

Cadillac had a successful formula it relentlessly pursued during good times and bad—except, significantly, during the 1980s when the marque faltered disastrously. It has spent the last fifteen years attempting to reconstitute itself in the wake of that fiasco and of repeated reorganizations that have taken the corporation far from Sloan's brilliant original vision.

In recent years, the division has settled on the "Art & Science" concept as the theme for Cadillac's future. Basically, this concept seeks to combine world-class technology with radical, geo-mechanical styling. The most notable single design cue has been the "shovel nose" or "cow catcher" grilles featured on all new Cadillac models. Incorporating the traditional egg crate design that dates back to 1931 or 1932, these grilles are bold—to put it mildly—and have put many people off. Still, it must be admitted that they are distinctive in the extreme.

1942 Series Sixty-Two.

Cadillacs are once again making unambiguous statements drawn straight from the brand's styling tradition.

Will it prove sufficient to save the brand? Only time will tell. In the meantime, this volume will tell you how Cadillac got itself into trouble in the first place and define in some detail what it is doing to revive its fortunes. One thing is certain: The next few years will be interesting ones in the luxury field.

CHAPTER ONE

1946 Series Sixty-Two sedan.

In the Beginning . . . :
1946–47

CADILLAC'S POSTWAR STORY really began at the depths of the Great Depression in May, 1934. That was when the decision was made to change strategic direction of the division with the appointment of a new general manager: Nicholas Dreystadt, formerly Cadillac's "works manager," i.e., manufacturing chief. His elevation was tacit admission by General Motors management that it was going to be essential to get control of manufacturing costs if Cadillac were to return to profitability and survive as a division.

The collapse of the stock market in October, 1929, came as a shock, and the collapsing automobile market that followed in 1930 as the Great Depression deepened only increased the sense of doom throughout industrial America. The luxury car manufacturers all came to more-or-less the same conclusion, i.e., that they needed more volume to survive and that moving down in price seemed to be the only way to achieve it.

The problem (only dimly realized by most) was that the traditional way of manufacturing luxury cars was so wildly inefficient it made building less expensive cars a practical impossibility. The Packard plant on East Grand Boulevard in Detroit and the Cadillac plant on Clark Street may have been top-notch by luxury producer standards, but they were practically Medieval in their operations compared to the state-of-the-art Ford production line across town at the Rouge.

In 1929, Ford had realized a unit profit of a mere $29 per car, a figure in line with Chevy and other volume producers at that end of the market, but recorded an impressive $48.9 million in profits overall because it built cars by the millions. Packard achieved a superficially impressive unit margin almost sixteen times as great—$458 per car on a fiscal year production of 53,537 cars—but only because it was able to jack-up its prices to cover its costs. Cadillac recorded a similar result: $268 per car on production of 36,598. The difference between the way in which the manufacturers behaved in the Ford class as compared to the Packard-Cadillac class cannot be over-stressed for it is central to an understanding of the agony all luxury car builders went through as they tried (and, in most cases, failed) to come to grips with the economic calamity that faced them.

The Ford car had to be built to a price and, in order to render it profitable at that low level, expenses had to be ferociously monitored. An old industry joke went that any competent engineer could design a water pump for a Rolls-Royce, but it took a genius to design one for a Ford or a Chevy. The meaning—which anyone in the industry understood without elaboration—was that the water pump for the Rolls-Royce only had to meet one criterion: it had to work. The water pump for the Ford or the Chevy, on the other hand, not only had to work, it had to be manufactured at the lowest possible unit cost.

The price of a Ford or a Chevy was dictated by the demands of the marketplace, and no manufacturer of low-priced cars could charge even $25 more than the market dictated without running the risk of disaster. Nor could money be saved by stripping content from the car, for it would then be uncompetitive for that reason. To put it another way, the manufacturer of low-priced cars could not cover its inefficiencies by arbitrarily raising prices to the consumer or by cheapening the product. That left only one solution: manufacturing costs had to be ruthlessly controlled.

The pre-Depression luxury market had been a different world. There, a difference in retail price of $25, or $50, or even a couple of hundred dollars had been meaningless. While it would be unfair to state that Cadillacs and Packards in the 1920s had been built without any thought to their costs, the Packard and Cadillac plants were pretty much run according to a sort of cost-plus pricing system. In other words, management tried as best it could to keep costs down, but, in the final analysis, whatever a Packard or Cadillac cost, something more was added for profit and that was the price quoted to the customer.

The approach worked well enough for many years because there was sufficient demand for damn-the-cost luxury rigs to support a practice that would have been lethal in the Ford class. The Depression brought the easy times to a crashing halt, though, and only when the luxury manufacturers, one by one, tried to build cars to a price did they come to grips with the dismal fact that —without exception—they really did not know how.

The experience of Packard in this regard is instructive—and it can be certain that Cadillac management was watching attentively. Packard management deduced that a major opening existed for luxury cars manufactured in the $1,500–$2,000 price range—about 20–30 percent below the traditional entry-level price. Packard's answer for the 1932 model year was the Series 900 Light Eight. A fine-looking car with a stylish and distinctive shovel-nose radiator, it was priced below $1,700.

And, in fact, the Light Eight sold extremely well—unfortunately, for it was bleeding the company dry and Packard management had to discontinue it within a few months. The company had lost a comparatively modest $119 on every car it built in 1931, but that figure soared to $601 on every car in 1932 when better than 73 percent of the volume was accounted for by the popular new series. (A total of 6,750 Light Eights were built, in all, between January and December.) Granted, 1932 was miserable year throughout the industry, but Packard's losses increased 47 percent faster than the losses across town at Cadillac, and the only significant difference between them was that Packard had tried its hand at building a car to a price in 1932 and Cadillac had not.

Not only did the Light Eight lose money on its own, it stole sales from the more profitable senior Packards, especially the Standard Eight that had been the volume mainstay. During 1932, Standard Eight sales all but evaporated as the public rushed to the new Light Eight. The following year, with sales still in the doldrums but with the Light Eight dead and buried and the Standard Eight (renamed the Eight) regaining momentum by default, Packard actually turned a profit of $37.53 per car.

Although the $355,714 it made does not seem like much, Packard was almost certainly the only American luxury car manufacturer to record a profit in 1933, and it was a remarkable achievement. In contrast, Cadillac posted a loss of $5.7 million, and the red ink at Lincoln amounted to more than $2.3 million. Meanwhile, Franklin, Marmon, Pierce-Arrow, and Stutz were all either in receivership or soon to be. Peerless had already quit the field entirely, although the company survived the Depression as the Peerless Brewing Company making Carling beer and Red Cap ale!

Still, Packard was hardly out of the woods. The Light Eight had unmistakably pointed the direction the company must follow. It had demonstrated something else, as well: that in order to follow the new direction Packard would have to learn how to build cars with a revolutionary level of efficiency. To that end, manufacturing expert George Christopher was hired away from General Motors. Christopher was given *carte blanche* to completely redesign the company's operations before it launched its next lower-priced car in 1935, the hugely successful One-Twenty.

Cadillac did not have to go outside the company for its miracle worker. Still, Nick Dreystadt was not, apparently, the type that made friends easily, and it does not seem that he made many during his dozen years at Cadillac. He was, however, tough as nails and determined to whip the division into line. Methodically, he went through the entire Cadillac operation, like some sort of Inspector General, looking for waste and inefficiency. Why did this part cost twice what a similar part cost? Were there not more efficient ways to do that assembly operation? Again and again, he forced his lieutenants to prove that the old ways of doing things were best—and, quite often, they weren't. When he was finished, the four-story Cadillac assembly operation had been consolidated into two. By all accounts, he succeeded brilliantly. If his harried associates never exactly learned to like him, they clearly learned to respect him and the job he was doing for the division.

As it turned out, 1936 was one of the most important years in the history of Cadillac. The cars were almost completely changed—including the use of modern technology not previously seen on Cadillacs—and, more importantly, the basic marketing strategy was revealed that would, in time, ensure the division's preeminence in the luxury field.

The key new product was the Series Sixty, the most affordable Cadillac since the earliest days, with a starting price of $1,645. The Series Sixty was actually positioned about 10 percent below the aborted 1932–33 Packard Light Eight, and matched almost exactly the price point of the 1934 La Salle. This, in turn, permitted the La Salle to ratchet itself down another notch to where the 1935 Packard One-Twenty had demonstrated the existence of a lucrative upper-medium-priced market. That the Series Sixty was "all Cadillac" and a true luxury car was undeniable, but, in order to reinvent the price/value relationships in the luxury field, new ways of doing business had been required. The most important development was the sharing of bodies with other General Motors product lines.

General Motors had started to rationalize its bodies in the early 1930s. Cadillac had some indirect credit for this, for it was Harley Earl's styling department that had convinced management it was unnecessary to use separate bodies with different General Motors brands in order to individualize them. Formerly, every division had developed its own body designs, but professional stylists could make any given body shell look like a Cadillac or a Buick, or whatever. The establishment of Art and Colour, to say nothing of the pressures exerted by collapsing sales, put irresistible pressure on the corporation to share bodies as a way to cut costs. By the end of the decade, General Motors volume lines were standardized on four basic body shells, designated "A," "B," "C," and "D," with some variants within these categories. The 1936 Cadillac Series Sixty shared the new General Motors B-body with the Buick Roadmaster. The closely related Series Seventy and Seventy-Five cars shared their bodies with the top-end Buick Limited, but benefited from Fleetwood interiors.

The Cadillac V8 lines not only got new bodies, they were given new powerplants. Cadillac introduced an entirely new engine family using modern technology to permit the blocks to be cast in one piece. This technology had been pioneered by Olds and Oakland in 1929–30, then developed further by Ford in 1932. Two Cadillac displacements were listed, 322 and 346 cubic inches. The Series Sixty received the former, the Series Seventy and Seventy-Five the latter. The only differences between the two engines were the bore and the horsepower. The 346 featured a one-eighth-inch larger bore; the 322 engine was rated at 125 horsepower at 3400 rpm, the 346 at 135. Both engines were designed by John F. Gordon, who had succeeded Owen Nacker, and was later to go on to a stellar career that included the general managership of Cadillac and the presidency of General Motors.

The 346 cubic inch version was destined to be the only engine used by Cadillac after 1940. In fact, it remained in use until the arrival of the legendary overhead valve V8 in 1949. This engine also deserves special mention for several other reasons. It used "pressed-in" piston rings that eventually became the standard throughout the industry. Its hydraulic valve lash adjustment was state-of-the-art. Although this feature had previously been used on the Cadillac V12 and V16 engines, it had never before been seen on a mass production engine. Two-barrel down draft carburetors of either Stromberg or Carter design were used, and also represented a major advance.

The news did not stop at the engine, either. There were numerous other technical refinements, some of them quite important. This was the first year with Cadillac for modern hydraulic brakes. In addition, spring rates were lowered to give a softer ride, the rear leaf springs were lubricated by wax-impregnated liners, and the 1936 V8 cars were the first Cadillacs to have a hypoid rear axle.

The most critically important achievement at Cadillac in 1936, however, was in marketing strategy. If Packard had shifted boldly into the medium-priced market with the One-Twenty series in 1935, it was mimicked by Lincoln when the Lincoln-Zephyr was announced in 1936. Both lines were competing against the LaSalle and neither were true luxury cars. The Series Sixty, in contrast, zeroed in on a viable market that was to become the volume end of the new luxury field. This was the big story of the decade insofar as the luxury business was concerned. Packard and Lincoln had given up the search, and opted to go after Buick and Chrysler in the upper-medium-priced market. Cadillac had tried a more conservative course and struck gold. Production of 1936 V8 models soared to 11,927, compared to 3,209 in 1935. Of this number, the Series Sixty accounted for 6,700 cars, the Seventy, 2,000, and the Seventy-Five, 3,227. It was a resounding success by any yardstick, and it pushed Cadillac to the top ranking in the luxury field where it was to reign supreme for decades to follow.

On the other hand, Packard reached its all-time production record of 122,593 cars in the 1937 model run. This achievement no doubt muted the cheering on Clark Street, but only 7,093 of those Packards were true luxury cars. In two years, Cadillac had moved so far ahead in the luxury field that it was now selling double the number of cars of its chief competitor.

Packard had also committed what later came to be regarded as a serious strategic blunder in the commercial car field. Commercial cars—hearses, ambulances, special limousines, and the like—comprised a small, but high-visibility, segment of the market. Packard, Cadillac, and the other remaining luxury brands all served this market with special, stretched-wheelbase chassis. Perhaps several thousand vehicles were produced per year, and Cadillac had decided to go after a bigger share of this business around 1935. Then, in 1936, Packard struck a deal with Henney, one of the builders, to supply the Packard chassis on an exclusive basis. It has been asserted for years that Packard delivered an ultimatum to the industry that Packard would no longer supply any builder who used the Cadillac chassis. According to this story, only Henney complied. The ultimatum story sounds ever so slightly illegal—restraint of trade, and all that—and another version of the story is that it was a shrewd deal that Henney had struck with Packard to get the drop on its competition. That it did, but what was in it for Packard is harder to figure. However it came to pass, Packard had shot itself in the foot. With Pierce-Arrow and Lincoln in rapid decline, the only source for commercial chassis for the entire industry (except, of course, for Henney) was suddenly Cadillac. As a result, Cadillac slowly, but surely, took over the industry and assumed a virtual monopoly on high-end commercial cars that lasted for half-a-century.[1]

There were a couple of major model developments at Cadillac in 1938, one of them among the most influential in Cadillac's history and the other—consuming similar amounts of energy and resources—with little long-term meaning whatsoever. The former was the Series Sixty Special, the latter was the second generation V16.

The Sixty Special is justifiably considered to be one of the most significant Cadillacs of all time. Cadillac publicity in later years glowingly described it as the "first practical motor car of advanced styling." This is the sort of overblown statement advertising departments seem to love to churn out. Apparently, they had forgotten the 1927 La Salle (among others). There are, however, two related reasons for the significance of the 1938 Sixty Special: one was its design; the other was the influence that design had.

The design of the Sixty Special was done principally by a young William Mitchell. Mitchell was later to rise to vice-president of design for General Motors, but he got his start as the first chief designer of the Cadillac studio in 1936. In the Sixty Special, he was heavily influenced by both the exciting Gordon Buehrig-designed Cord 810/812, and an earlier French design for the 1934 Panhard Panoramique. The basic grille design, with its bold horizontal bars that swept around to each side, had appeared on the Cord in 1936. The roofline, in turn, was inspired by the Panhard. This is not in any way to de-

1938 Sixty-Special.

tract from Mitchell's achievement, of course, but merely to note that automotive designers are influenced by each other, as is the case with artists in any field. Great art is not created in a void—and the Sixty Special was a genuine work of art.

Perhaps the most interesting feature of the Sixty Special was the way its greenhouse seemed to rest on the lower body. The Panhard had been inspired by the intimacy of the deluxe railway carriages of the day, whose windows—with the roof flowing down between them—rested on broad sills. The result seemed to Harley Earl to suggest the intimacy of a convertible sedan, and it was this idea that he communicated to Mitchell. The Sixty Special, as it was finalized, had very much the sporty appearance of a hardtop convertible, though long before the term was coined. The hood line swept back and merged with the beltline roll that formed the exterior sill for the side windows, and then flowed on back to an extended rear deck. In that, the Sixty Special was the first production car from a major manufacturer to have what would later become known as "notchback" styling, with a long, and fully integrated, trunk. Further, because the car was arrestingly low by the standards of the day, no running boards were needed. The total package was wonderfully exciting and youthful—a true sport sedan for the emerging executive class.

As the prototype was significantly smaller than even the smaller Cadillacs of the time, the initial plan was to build it as a La Salle Fifty Special. Production cost estimates reportedly ruled that out, so the Fifty became a Sixty, and Cadillac made history with perhaps the first successful personal luxury car. The Sixty Special exerted enormous influence on the industry (Studebaker, Nash, and Packard late-prewar products, in particular) as well as on General Motors, and it became the design prototype for nearly every major General Motors product built during the next dozen years.

Cadillac model designations were modified for 1938. Starting at the bottom, they became the Sixty-One, Sixty Special, Sixty-Five, Seventy-Five, and Ninety (V16).

The 1939 model range was a general continuation of that offered in 1938. There were no engineering developments of note, but the Sixty-Five was dropped in favor of the Sixty Special, and the Sixty-One got a new body. The Sixty Special was available with an optional sun roof.

By this time, Packard management, finally appreciating what Cadillac was up to, got a new Super Eight into production in the emerging volume luxury market first discovered by the Series Sixty in 1936. It was a bit late, though, as Cadillac already had a solid head start in exploiting the new market and was, by this point, the clear leader in the luxury field.

It has long been said that the reason for Packard's collapse in the luxury market was the One-Twenty (and its even cheaper stable mate, the One-Ten). The old saw has it that when wealthy Packard owners saw their chauffeurs arriving for work in their new One-Twenties, the senior Packards were doomed. To this writer, this has always seemed an over-simplification. Consider the Lincoln-Zephyr. It was a direct competitor of the One-Twenty, and had the added burden of a seriously tarnished image due to its antiquated mechanicals and underdeveloped V12. Yet, Lincoln survived as a credible luxury nameplate. If the Zephyr could not destroy Lincoln's reputation, nothing the One-Twenty (which was, by all accounts, a very good car) did to Packard's reputation was beyond remedy.

The better explanation is that Packard ignored a major shift in the market and paid the price. When Cadillac introduced the Series Sixty in 1936, they were the first competitor in what proved to be the new volume end of the luxury field. Just as Packard had gotten there first in the 1920s and left Cadillac scrambling to keep pace, so Cadillac did it to Packard in the 1930s. Between 1936 and 1938, Cadillac introduced a steady stream of important product lines to exploit this new market segment: the Sixty, Sixty-Five, Sixty Special, Seventy, and Seventy-Five. Packard had no counter whatsoever until the Super Eight was repositioned in 1939, did not have anything like a full range of competitive vehicles until 1940, and never answered the challenge posed by the highly successful Sixty Special. The simple truth is that Packard management sat back and did nothing for several crucial years while Cadillac ate their lunch. In any industry, a failure to move aggressively to exploit market developments has serious consequences.

In fairness to Packard management, the tremendous success of the One-Twenty clearly clouded their thinking. In 1936, for example, Packard built 55,042 One-Twenties. In contrast, Cadillac built 6,700 Series Sixties. The Series Sixty must have seemed like small potatoes to Packard's management. And, it was small potatoes. The luxury market was still reeling from the effects of the Depression, but, when the market started to come back around 1940, Cadillac was firmly positioned to reap the benefits and Packard was not.

Announced in October, 1939, the 1940 Cadillacs were continuations of the successful models of the previous year. The Sixty-Two was mounted on the new General Motors C-body, which would continue over after the war, also used by La Salle, Buick, Olds, and Pontiac for their mid- or top-range models. Although inspired by the highly influential Sixty Special, the C-body was softer and more fluid in its lines. Initially, it was available in sedan and coupe body types, but, in mid-year, convertible and convertible sedan variants were offered, as well. In the view of most observers, the C-body was one of the most pleasing designs of the era.

The Sixty Special continued to use an exclusive body. This year, a divider was offered that turned it into a short-wheelbase limousine called the Town Car. In general, Cadillac styling in 1940 was a continuation of the 1939 design with minor modifications, the major one being the grille. It was made bolder in order to facilitate recognition at a distance. Sealed beam headlights were new, as well, and were one of the first examples of government-mandated equipment regulations. This was also the first year for turn indicators as standard equipment, and the last year for sidemounts as an option.

For Cadillac, 1941 represented its prewar high watermark as an auto producer. After years of struggling, everything finally came together in one glorious year. The number of Cadillac product lines was up at the same time the number of individual models was substantially reduced. Most of the model reduction was a result of the phase-out of the V16, but the Seventy-Two was dropped, as well. The series designations for 1941 consisted of Sixty-One, Sixty-Two, Sixty-Three, Sixty Special, Sixty-Seven, and Seventy-Five. The first four were standardized on a 126-inch chassis, while the Sixty-Seven and

1941 Series Sixty-Two convertible sedan.

Seventy-Five used 138 inches and 136 inches, respectively. As with the 1940 Seventy-Two, the Sixty-Seven shared a Fisher body with the Buick Limited. As before, the reason for the existence of two ranges of long-wheelbase sedans in the Cadillac line-up was difficult to fathom, but the Sixty-Seven did offer a more stylish alternative to the rather severe Seventy-Five. On the other hand, the Seventy-Five offered the cachet and deluxe appointments of a Fleetwood-crafted body.

The Series Sixty-One replaced the La Salle, that nameplate having been retired at the close of the 1940 model run. It was built on the new General Motors B-body, which was shared by every General Motors car division save Chevrolet, but it was a large and entirely suitable body for an entry-level Cadillac series. It was available in two- and four-door fastback styles. The Sixty-Two continued over from 1940 with trim modifications; the Sixty-Two convertible sedan was now the only such body style available from Cadillac. The Sixty-Three, for its part, was essentially a six-window version of the C-body sedan for buyers who preferred that style.

For the first time in many years, all Cadillac-built cars shared the same basic engine and drivetrain in 1941. The V8 was increased in horsepower to 150 and, according to contemporary reports, delivered a remarkable combination of power, flexibility, and smoothness, even by the high standards of the luxury field. Top speed was estimated at 100 mph, while 0 to 60 acceleration was estimated at 14 seconds—remarkable in 1941. Adding to the benefits of being a Cadillac owner was another landmark development: Hydra-Matic. This was the first truly practical, fully-automatic transmission ever offered. It had appeared on Oldsmobile in 1940, and proved especially successful and popular as mated to the Cadillac V8.

Prices started at $1,445, a remarkably modest price for a car with the Cadillac nameplate attached, and sales responded accordingly. In fact, 1941 was far and away the best model year in Cadillac history up to that time. A grand total of 66,130 cars were built during the model run.

The 1942 models were extensively restyled for Cadillac's Fortieth Anniversary. Most obvious was the new pontoon fender design that, thanks to fender caps, swept into the front doors (except on the Seventy-Five). Wheelbases were changed to 129 inches (Sixty-One, Sixty-Two, and Sixty-Three), 133 inches (Sixty-Special), and 136 inches (Sixty-Seven and Seventy-Five). For the Sixty Special, the 1942 model represented a basic conceptual change; the trim sport sedan of 1938–41 was supplanted by a long-wheelbase flagship that would, henceforth, carry the nameplate. Meanwhile, the Cadillac open car line-up was reduced to one, the Sixty-Two convertible (which featured rear side windows for the first time). The grilles were new and much bolder than in 1941, while still continuing the "tombstone" treatment. Interiors were completely redone, as well. They were very pleasing cars, but destined to have a short run.

The nation had been shifting over to a war footing ever since hostilities began in Europe in the latter months of 1939. By the time the 1942 Cadillacs were being readied for production in the summer of 1941, it was obvious to most Americans that the war in Europe would eventually involve the United States in a direct way.[2] It was not known what the entry of the United States into a full-fledged war would mean to Cadillac and to the auto industry, but the impact was already being felt in the scramble for scarce items and the need to find suitable substitutes for a growing list of strategic materials that the American government ordered reserved for military application. There was, in fact, considerable concern among prospective car buyers regarding the effect of all these substitutions and shortages on the quality of the soon-to-be-introduced 1942 models. It was widely believed they would be inferior to the 1941 models, but history proved these fears misplaced, as hundreds of thousands of 1942 cars from all manufacturers gave excellent service during the critical time approaching.

The government in Washington, for its part, was taking great pains to demonstrate its ability to sow confusion with some of its regulations regarding allocations and restrictions. By the latter months of 1941, when production cutbacks began to bite and total war seemed ever more imminent, almost literally anything on wheels could be sold to an increasingly car hungry public—"desperate" might more accurately describe the mood. Nonetheless, the government became fearful for the fate of certain manufacturers who had been unable to obtain adequate quantities of scarce chrome. Accordingly, it drastically restricted the use of chrome by all manufacturers so no company would have an "unfair" competitive advantage. General Motors divisions, which had ample supplies of chrome trim parts already on hand, were actually forced to paint over the chrome before they could use the parts.

The "blackout" car was developed to deal with chrome shortages, both real and government-fantasized. The regulations specified that most normally chromed trim parts, except bumpers, would have to be painted on cars built after December 15, 1941. Each manufacturer handled this on an individual basis. Some developed a series of two-tone schemes to try to dress up the chromeless cars as much as possible (with the painted trim parts harmonizing with, or contrasting to, the body color), while others just got as close to chrome color as they could by painting it all gray. Surviving factory photos of actual blackout 1942 Cadillacs show the chrome-gray scheme.

The War Production Board had come into being in 1940 in order to regulate American industry in anticipation of the coming emergency. General Motors' president, William S. Knudsen, was chosen to direct it. On September 13, 1941, the government established quotas by manufacturer for civilian passenger car production in the August–November period. On October 24th, December quotas were issued. January and February, 1942, quotas were subsequently issued, then repeatedly reduced. On December 24th, as a conservation measure, it was forbidden to equip cars with spare tires.

Effective January 1, 1942, civilian sales of passenger cars was halted pending establishment of a rationing system, although production continued under strict quotas for each manufacturer. On January 6th, the manufacture of antifreeze was prohibited. On January 14th, the rationing of tires at the retail level was ordered. By the time February 10th was set as the date for final production of passenger cars, it was a struggle to keep the lines going. On January 24th, Willys-Overland was the first manufacturer to cease production. Dodge followed on the 29th, while Lincoln, Chrysler, and Studebaker stopped the lines on the 31st. Olds, Buick, Cadillac, Hudson, and Nash lasted until February 3rd. Chevrolet quit on the 6th. Ford and Packard made it all the way to the 9th. The last 1942 Pontiac—apparently the final 1942 American car—rolled off

1942 Series Sixty-Two convertible.

the line on February 10, 1942. It would be nearly four years before the volume manufacture resumed.

A mere 16,511 Cadillacs were built during the 1942 model run. As soon as the last one came off the line, the giant Clark Street plant was reconverted for war work. For the next three years, the men and women of Cadillac devoted all their energies to government war assignments, and compiled a truly enviable record in that regard.

The American automobile industry confidently anticipated the return to a peacetime economy. It did so with an optimism born of the tremendous achievements accomplished during the war and of the certain knowledge that a prosperous nation, deprived of cars for nearly four years, eagerly awaited the chance to buy automobiles again. As early as 1944, with war assignments beginning to wind down, the Government had given the industry permission to begin planning for the resumption of civilian production. It would be a daunting task, one as difficult as the shift to war assignments had been in 1942, but the men and women of Cadillac were determined to approach it with the skill and dedication they demonstrated in completing so many equally difficult wartime assignments.

If there were to be many obstacles to Cadillac's postwar plans, the division would also receive an unexpected—but enormously important—bonus: Packard management decided not to resume production of a full range of senior cars. Packard's focus on its medium-priced lines, apparent before the war, came to full fruition in 1946. In fact, the 1942 senior body dies had been sold to the Soviet Government during the war, so while the 1942 senior Packard emerged

1946 Series Sixty-Two.

as socialist executive transportation half a world away, Packard elected to rely upon the smaller Clipper body for its entire postwar effort.

To be sure, the Clipper body was modern and handsome, and had considerable potential, but little effort was made to upgrade it so as to offer a meaningful challenge to Cadillac. Two token Custom Super models (a sedan and a coupe) were all that were offered in the Cadillac model range, and, even then, they weren't placed into production until May, 1946, in order that the company could concentrate on its mid-range models. Late in the 1946 model run, a well-executed long wheelbase line introduced for seven-passenger sedan and limousine application showed what could have been done. For a time, Packard was destined to return to something like its prewar impact in that prestigious market sub-segment, but Packard management had clearly made the fateful decision to turn its back on luxury cars as the mainstay of its corporate strategy.

Meanwhile, Lincoln planned to continue to produce cars at the lower fringe of the luxury segment. The Zephyr name was not revived after the war, although the model range and the largely discredited Lincoln V12 engine were little changed. The Custom limousines were gone, however, and so the Continental, which would continue to be built in small numbers, would constitute Ford Motor Company's only presence in the true luxury field. Ford, at least, was thinking ahead and planning a major assault on Cadillac with the all-new postwar Lincoln being readied for the 1949 model year.

Chrysler, as before the war, intended to build a few long wheelbase Imperial seven-passenger sedans and limousines, while the eccentric (if highly collectible) Town and Country series would offer an interesting alternative to

1946 Series Seventy-Five.

1946 Series Sixty-One interior.

luxury buyers who wished to return to the days of wood body construction. Few would avail themselves of the opportunity, proving once again that a car can be a marketing disappointment when new and still become enormously popular with latter-day collectors.

If Chrysler had never had much of a presence in the luxury market, and thus can be excused for not setting its sights a little higher, the inability of Packard management to comprehend the importance of maintaining a convincing presence in the luxury field after the war is extremely difficult to comprehend. Packard had, second only to Cadillac, the largest prewar customer base in the field. In 1946, Packard probably could have locked in a 25–30% market share for the asking in this highly profitable segment. Ten years later, this would have translated into perhaps 50,000 units—more than Packard production in medium and luxury fields combined by that point—and would have left Packard a strong and viable company in the shake-out destined to deplete the ranks of the independents in the 1950s. Many historians have fingered this decision as the proximate cause of Packard's demise as an auto producer. In 1951, when James J. Nance signed on as Packard's new president and set about reestablishing the company's presence in the luxury field, he found to his dismay that it was already too late to break Cadillac's lock.

For whatever reason, Packard management was asleep at the switch and, had they been in Cadillac's pay, it is hard to see how they could have done more to help their arch-rival across town. As a consequence of their default, and of the tepid efforts at Lincoln and Chrysler, Cadillac was left virtually alone with a full range of luxury products as the new era dawned. The significance of this development on Cadillac's postwar prominence cannot be over-stated.

The difficult process of restarting the passenger car production lines began in March, 1944, when the War Production Board appointed a committee of manufacturers' representatives to plan for peacetime conversion. At Cadillac, as at all the other companies, there was no thought of producing an entirely new postwar car; there was no time to plan, develop, design, engineer, and test one. Not that anyone would care; pent-up consumer demand was in the millions. Anything that rolled would sell in 1946, 1947, and, probably, 1948, as well.

On May 11, 1945, the War Production Board announced that it would per-

1947 Series Sixty-Two convertible.

mit manufacturers to begin reconversion to civilian production on July 1st. Gasoline rationing officially ended on August 15th and, on that same date, the War Production Board lifted all restrictions on civilian passenger car production. The race was on.

Ford actually managed to build its first 1946 car on July 3rd, and another 359 cars by the end of the month, although they must have been assembled largely from leftover 1942 parts and supplies. Ford could not have reconverted the giant Rouge plant in two days, and the first new Fords were not exhibited to the public until October. The second manufacturer to begin 1946 production, Hudson, did not get the lines going until August 30th. The first 1946 General Motors product, a Chevrolet, didn't see the light of day until October 3rd, followed by limited initial Pontiac production the following day. Cadillac finally got the production lines running on October 17th.

Unfortunately, everything came to a grinding halt for General Motors before it had really commenced. On November 21st the UAW struck with a job action that became the longest in General Motors history and which was not settled until March 13, 1946. Chevrolet production resumed on March 29th and all other General Motors divisions resumed production by April 1st.

The first 1946 Cadillacs were little changed from those that had last rolled off the line in 1942. Styling alterations were limited to details. New hood and deck emblems were composed of a dramatic "V" in which nested the Cadil-

1947 Sixty-Special.

lac crest, and the position of the parking lights was changed. Cadillac simplified its model line-up, too. The Series Sixty-Three and Sixty-Seven lines were eliminated, probably under the pressure of capacity restrictions. The Sixty-Seven body had been shared with the Buick Limited before the war and Buick did not revive that series, either. In any case, the Sixty-Three and Sixty-Seven had always seemed somewhat superfluous at Cadillac and it is doubtful their absence was regretted by many—or even noticed. Other than that, the model range offered was essentially the same as that listed before the war halted civilian production.

If styling alterations were minor, engineering changes in 1946 were almost non-existent. Cadillac could—and did—promote its V8 as "battle-proved" on the grounds that it (owing to wartime demand for military applications) was one of the few automotive powerplants to be produced and improved without interruption during the war. The same held true for Hydra-Matic. In fact, Cadillac ad writers may have done too good a job of making the point. Numerous complaints began to flow into Clark Street headquarters from dealers and individuals who had purchased surplus military engines and transmissions, and attempted to convert them for civilian use. Dealers were sent an urgent bulletin warning them that "the purchase of such materials should not be encouraged," and went on to relate a litany of horror stories:

An owner of a past series Cadillac had an M-24 tank engine and Hydra-

1947 Series Sixty-Two coupe.

Matic installed in his car, and after the installation had been completed, he found that the car could not be backed up because there was no reverse unit in the transmission. A sawmill operator installed a tank engine and Hydra-Matic as the power unit in his small sawmill. This man wanted to know how to eliminate the downshift of the transmission with resultant changes in saw speed every time the saw struck a knot in the green lumber being cut.[3]

The big problem for Cadillac in 1946, though, was just getting the cars out the door. Every manufacturer had planned for spectacular levels of production and had stumbled over the same obstacles of shortages, labor unrest, and allocation restrictions. In light of what it had to overcome, Cadillac management was no doubt grateful for the 29,194 cars actually built in the stop-and-go 1946 model run—even if it was a far cry from the 100,000 cars the division had confidently predicted in the summer of 1945. One thing that had expanded sharply in 1946, however, was the price of a new Cadillac. Despite government price controls, the least expensive Cadillac now listed for $1,920, and would not remain at even that level for very long.

On July 1, 1946, Nicholas Dreystadt moved on, following a dramatically successful dozen years at Cadillac's helm. He was reassigned to Chevrolet, then fell ill with cancer and died two years later. His replacement at Cadillac was chief engineer John F. Gordon, who had designed the current Cadillac L-head V8 and played a major role in the landmark overhead-valve V8 then under development. Gordon was replaced as chief engineer by another rising star, Edward N. Cole.

The 1947 model year saw Cadillacs that were mildly facelifted, but only in trim details. A newly designed Cadillac crest emblem was featured, while "Cadillac" appeared in script on the front fenders, and the grille had four horizontal bars instead of the previous five. Such were the cosmic changes for 1947.

Few manufacturers expended much effort on new models in this era. Selling them was not a problem. The focus was on building them, and the next two model years were spent trying to increase output to satisfy the seemingly insatiable demands of the marketplace in the face of repeated interruptions. General Motors plants were idled again and again in 1947 because of strikes and shortages in various critical supplies, such as steel. In June, 1948, General Motors was shut down due to a coal strike. If it was not one thing, it was something else.

Nevertheless, Cadillac production managed to approach the prewar level in 1947. As in 1946, the great majority of Cadillacs built were Sixty-Twos. Even the prewar level of production was not enough, though, in these car-hungry times, and the division ended the year with over 96,000 unfilled orders. Still, a remarkable total of 61,926 cars were turned out. Or, perhaps it was not so remarkable. As it was reported at the time, a decision had been made by General Motors management to divert a disproportionate share of the corporation's scarce materials allocations to Cadillac on the belief that, if production was going to be restricted, materials might as well go where they would produce the most revenue.

CHAPTER TWO

Cadillac's one millionth car comes off the line in 1949.

1,000,000 *th* CADILLAC NOV. 25, 1949

The Tail Fin Era:
1948–49

THE FIRST ALL-NEW postwar Cadillacs appeared in February, 1948. Although the model line-up was identical to that offered in 1948, and the Seventy-Five range was carried over unchanged on its prewar body shell, the rest of the Cadillac line was breathtakingly new.

While cleaner and more streamlined in their looks, the most notable design feature of the 1948s—and the one that instantly caught the public's fancy —was the small tail fin at the tip of each rear fender. The tail fins housed the taillights and, on the left fin, the taillight flipped up to reveal the gas tank filler pipe. It was a clever arrangement, but the most important benefit accruing from the new design was the wider body that afforded significantly increased interior room, despite the fact the new cars were slightly shorter and somewhat lighter in weight than they had been before.

As was the case with so much early postwar design from all manufacturers, the tail fin had been inspired by military experience. In Cadillac's case, the direct inspiration was the Lockheed P-38 Lightning fighter plane. Harley Earl and a group of his designers had seen it before the war and experimented with a host of aircraft-type design motifs. The team that designed the first "tail fin era" Cadillac was headed by Franklin Quick Hershey, and its development was fairly convoluted. Hershey recalled:

One day the boss [Harley Earl] took us out to one of the airfields—this was about 1941 or '42—and they had a lot of airplanes there. I saw the P-38 and that gave me the idea to put its fin on the rear fender.

The actual design of the 1948 Cadillac was not undertaken until after the war, though. When he was given the assignment, Frank Hershey and his team worked under the added burden of the lengthy UAW strike in the winter of 1945–46:

> The design department had to go out on strike. So, we moved the whole Cadillac studio out to the basement of a farm I had out in Michigan—the Walker Mill Farm. And, we spent four or five months in my basement and did the '48 Cadillac.[1]

The tail fin was not, however, instantly popular with General Motors' management. Again, Hershey recalls an incident that took place after the 1948 design had been completed and the 1949 model-year revision was just getting under way:

> A lot of people were wary of it. I was working on the full-size clay model and we were working to change the front end for the next year. This was just after the strike. Harley came up with Dreystadt and they said, "Boy, take the fin off! Take it off right now! Nobody likes it! Take it off!" I had the whole thing covered with a piece of canvas because we were working up front. I didn't take it off. And, Harley came up about two days later, and he said, "Goddamn it, I told you to take that damn thing off! If it isn't off tomorrow, I'm going to fire you." This is the way he talked. I didn't take it off. About two days after that, he came up with the service manager, the advertising manager and so on, and

1948 Series Sixty-Two coupe.

said, "Look, did you take the fin off?" And, I said, "No." He laughed, "Oh, thank God—everybody loves it! Leave it on!"[2]

The 1948 interior was highlighted by a particularly beautiful instrument panel which Cadillac described as, "revolutionary in concept and the ultimate in functional design." The main instruments and controls were all grouped directly in front of the driver in a large pod that jutted out from the panel, and included the gauge cluster, as well as controls for air vents and windshield wipers, and the hand brake and hood lock lever, for good measure.

Cadillac was also selected to participate in an important experiment that year. Semon E. Knudsen was the son of former General Motors' president William S. Knudsen and was destined to be the future general manager of Pontiac and Chevrolet. In that slot, he developed the "Wide Track" theme that really got Pontiac rolling in the late-1950s. In 1948, he was achieving something of a reputation within the corporation for his expertise in machine tools, as they related to manufacturing. Knudsen recalled:

> I went down to a staff job, which was located at Cadillac. It was a program
> that had been developed by the corporation to either improve the quality of
> some particular operation or mechanize the operation. When I got there,
> they were just doing a kind of research job. I had been in the machine tool
> business. So, I set up a sales organization and I went out to the plants—all
> the GM plants—looked around and figured what needed to be done and I
> gave them an estimate on it like a machine tool builder.[3]

Knudsen's modest description hardly does the program justice. In fact, it was the early conceptual effort at General Motors to develop automation, and

1948 Sixty Special.

to figure out how to spread its benefits throughout the corporation. All the robotics and state-of-the-art computerized manufacturing systems being used today are the spiritual descendants of that embryonic program started at Cadillac in 1948. It is significant that Cadillac (and, not incidentally, Knudsen) was chosen to do this early work.

Production in 1948 dipped to 52,706 cars, owing to the short model year (nine months as opposed to the thirteen-month run of the 1947 models). Overall market share increased slightly, but Cadillac's share of the market segment made up of the major luxury brands, particularly, declined sharply, from 42.6 percent to 34.9 percent. There is considerable evidence that this decline set in motion a chain of events that would dramatically effect future Cadillac product development. To understand this, a little explanation is in order.

Packard created something of a stir in the middle of 1947 when it made an early announcement of its 1948 line with its first postwar convertible. Billed as "all-new" cars, the 1948 Packards were, in fact, thinly reskinned editions of the 1941 Clipper, involving new outer sheetmetal on hoods, fenders, and doors. The new look, termed "Free Flow" styling in Packard advertising, was the first example from a major manufacturer of what eventually came to be called "bathtub" design, and it immediately caught the public's fancy.

The "1949" Lincolns were introduced in April of 1948—within a few weeks of the 1948 Cadillacs—and instantly captured the public's fancy, as well. Their styling—done during the war by E. T. Gregorie, Edsel Ford's original Ford Mo-

1948 Series Sixty Special as custom-fitted by Derham.

The stillborn 1949 Seventy-Five.

tor Company styling chief—was every bit as radical a bathtub design as the
Packard, perhaps more so. Worse, from Cadillac's perspective, was the new Lincoln Cosmopolitan series, priced head-to-head against the volume Sixty-Two.

The deficiencies of Cadillac's main competitors, Packard and Lincoln, have
been pointed out repeatedly in this book, particularly the fact that, by the
1940s, most of the cars these "competitors" built were not actually positioned
in the Cadillac price class at all. At the time, however, Packard and Lincoln
were still considered luxury nameplates—not as prestigious as Cadillac, perhaps, but better than the mid-priced brands against which most Packards and
Lincolns were actually sold. There is anecdotal evidence to support the view
that Cadillac management regarded Packard and Lincoln in much the same
way, i.e., as the direct competition. In that, they were not alone.

Packard and Lincoln had been top-rated luxury cars until the mid-1930s.
Since that time, their share of the true luxury market had gone into precipitous
decline. In 1947, Cadillac probably outsold the two combined by a margin of
about four-to-one when genuine luxury cars are considered. Yet, nearly everyone in the industry continued to regard Cadillac, Packard, and Lincoln as direct competitors—this despite the fact that, in the true luxury market, Cadillac outsold Packard and Lincoln by a huge margin, and despite the fact that a
solid majority of the cars Packard and Lincoln built (in Lincoln's case, nearly all
of them) were mid-priced cars that sold for substantially less than any Cadillac.[4]

So, Packard and Lincoln scored major sales gains versus Cadillac in 1948 at
the same time they introduced the first examples of a dramatic new styling
school. When, at the same time Lincoln showed signs of a serious move into
the volume Cadillac class, it caused a stir on Clark Street that would have major implications down the road.

In the meantime, the Cadillac range for 1949, as has already been noted,
was only modestly restyled. The most obvious alteration was the bolder grille

1949 Series Sixty-One sedan.

that wrapped around the front fenders to the wheel openings. Inside, the lovely control pod design of 1948 was radically revised to eliminate the pod, and recess all of the gauges and controls into the instrument panel proper. It was not nearly so appealing a design in the opinion of many, but it was far more conventional.

The model line-up at the start of the year was identical to that offered in 1948, even including the prewar Seventy-Fives, now looking very venerable, indeed. A replacement on the postwar body shell was planned but never built, and more of this aborted program will be discussed later.[5]

A really significant addition to the line came in mid-year with the first two-door hardtop, the Coupe de Ville. Cadillac, Buick, and Olds all got to use this C-Body hardtop in 1949, although it was actually designed by Ned Nickles at Buick as early as 1945. A total of 9,499 were built in all, including 2,150 Coupe de Villes, 3,006 Oldsmobile Holidays, and 4,343 Buick Rivieras. The new body style swept the industry, and, within two or three years, virtually every manufacturer was offering it.[6]

If the advent of the hardtop was a landmark design development, there was equally significant news on the engineering front. Cadillac announced what it rightly regarded as one of greatest engineering achievements to date in its new short stroke, high compression, overhead-valve V8. This engine represented a genuine advance in technology. Together with a similar engine introduced concurrently by Oldsmobile, it is considered a true landmark engine design, one that influenced the entire industry and whose influence is still felt today. If the V8 is the quintessential American powerplant type, then the 1949 Cadillac example was truly a historic event.

Research on the engine had begun in 1936 when Ernest W. Seaholm was chief engineer. Through the years of development, men who played critical roles included John F. Gordon, chief engineer following Seaholm and general manager in 1948 when the new engine was introduced, Edward N. Cole, who followed Gordon as chief engineer, and Harry Barr, who was the "engineer in charge of engines"—a title that has always delighted this writer.

Seaholm, Gordon, and Cole all saw the future direction toward lighter, more powerful, high-compression engines. In part, this was in the expectation—widely shared throughout the industry—that increasingly better grades of fuel would make higher compression engines both possible and, because they were possible (and would, therefore, be built by Cadillac's competitors), necessary. A Cadillac promotional booklet issued at the time the engine was introduced to the public stated, "Starting literally with an idea, plus the finest engine experience in the world, the Cadillac engineering design staff set about creating the ideal future engine." Once again, Cadillac's advertising writers were unable to improve on reality, for that was a pretty fair statement of what actually happened.

From 1936 to late 1941, experiments had been made with variety of engine types. By the time World War II interrupted the effort, several experimental models had been built. After the Japanese surrendered in the summer of 1945, work resumed in earnest. Between 1946 and 1948, more than 25 engines were built and tested—the engine, in its final form, being tested well over 1,000,000 miles. The combined features of the new engine resulted in 12 percent less cylinder wall area with a consequent reduction in heat loss, improved cooling efficiency, and 20 percent less piston travel, among other benefits. Taken to-

1949 Coupe de Ville.

Top, 1949 Series Sixty-Two convertible; *bottom*, 1949 Series Sixty-Two sedan.

gether, the combination of high thermal and mechanical efficiency produced both greatly increased power output and economy. The new engine was also substantially lighter in weight.

The 1949 Cadillac V8 was an engineering grand slam and immediately made obsolete the engines used by all of its luxury market competitors. Packard and Chrysler were still running L-head-type straight eights, although Chrysler was hard at work on its own high compression V8. Lincoln had just introduced a new V8 for its 1949 models, but it, too, was of the antiquated L-head design and was hardly more advanced than the 1948 engine Cadillac had just abandoned. In the marketplace, the bloom was quickly off the rose of the 1949 Lincoln, dogged as it was by quality control problems, particularly with its engine. The announcement of the Cadillac overhead-valve V8 only made matters worse.

Cadillac did face a new competitive challenge in 1949, if only in embryonic form. A Chrysler Imperial four-door sedan was offered for the first time since the war in what was destined to become a major effort to launch the Imperial as a full-fledged luxury brand. In 1949, however, the effort did not amount to much. Production is not known, and how anybody found out about the new car is anybody's guess (the Imperial sedan wasn't even listed in the catalog). Assuming they did, they probably were not terribly impressed. Chrysler styling, which was new for 1949, was disastrously out of sync with the times. While everyone else was building cars that were lower and sleeker, the entire 1949 Chrysler corporate range was high and narrow and, in basic configuration, more closely resembled the General Motors designs of 1939 than the state-of-the-art ones a decade later. It was a conservative attitude regarding design that was to cost Chrysler dearly in the next several years, in general, and severely hamper their ability to develop the Imperial nameplate, in particular. So, that made one less competitor for Cadillac to worry about—at least for the time being.

All in all, 1949 was a perfectly splendid year for Cadillac. As if the division needed anything else to celebrate, the one-millionth car—a Coupe de Ville— was produced on November 25, 1949.

Top, 1949 Sixty-Special instrument panel; *bottom*, 1949 engine.

CHAPTER THREE

The body drop at the Clark Street plant in 1952.

Of Tail Fins and Bathtubs: 1950–53

THE 1950 MODEL RUN was another landmark year as Cadillac production exceeded 100,000 cars for the first time in the division's history. This was achieved despite a paring down of the line-up from 12 models to nine. All of the model deletions came in the new Seventy-Five Series, primarily through elimination of the old "business" models sold to professional users (funeral homes, limousine livery services, and the like). Hardtop styling, pioneered the previous year, replaced the pillared coupe entirely in the new line-up. In addition to the Sixty-Two Coupe de Ville, there was a standard Sixty-Two hardtop, and a hardtop in the Sixty-One line, as well. This gave Cadillac yet another important edge over competitive luxury brands, none of whom had any hardtops at all. In fact, the entire industry was taken totally unawares by the General Motors hardtops. In the luxury field, Imperial and Packard did not even try to respond to the challenge—this was the final year for the prewar Packard body, in any event—while Lincoln rushed a fancy pillared coupe (the Cosmopolitan Capri) into production to offer at least some sort of counter to the threat. It is unlikely that it had much effect.

Although the Cadillac bodies in 1950 looked entirely new, they were not. A close examination under the skin reveals that they were, in fact, heavily reworked versions of the 1948 B- and C-bodies.[1] A significant feature of the new design was the one-piece, curved windshield. The dramatic egg crate grille was a stylistic development of the theme Cadillac had been using since 1942 and, in general, there was little in the 1950 styling that was really new in the conceptual sense. It was just a fresh—and successful—variation on the same proven themes.

The program of product rationalization begun at General Motors in the early 1930s came to full flower in this era, and this played a big part in the entire B- and C-body programs. Every General Motors division, except Chevrolet (which only had one body to start with), was reduced to one basic body shell between 1949 and 1951. Pontiac dropped from two to one. Olds, Buick, and Cadillac went from three to one (or, four to one in Cadillac's case, depending on how body shells are interpreted).

From 1949, Pontiac and Chevrolet shared the A-body, and had it as an exclusive by 1951, while Olds used only the B-body from mid-1951. Buick and Cadillac technically had B- and C-bodies from 1950, but, as had been the case since 1948, the new C-body was a stretched derivative of the B-body. The C-Special used by the Cadillac Sixty Special was, in turn, a stretched version of the C-body. Even the Seventy-Fives were brilliantly engineered off the B/C-body. The rear quarters interchanged with the Coupe de Ville, the rear doors were slightly reworked from the Sixty Special, and only the roof was a unique stamping. It was one of the cleverest design tricks ever, and set a standard for limousine design that would endure for years to come.

1950 Sixty Special.

Why was General Motors so anxious to simplify its product lines? The answer was simple: cost. The corporation's management, still guided by the legendary Alfred P. Sloan, had been genuinely taken aback by the dramatic price inflation that occurred as soon as price controls were eased at the end of the war. There were many in General Motors leadership—Sloan among them—who were haunted by the sharp recession that had followed the last world war. In that economic crisis, General Motors itself had come close to ruin. So, although there was a huge pent-up demand for cars in first years after the war, Sloan and his colleagues knew that sooner or later supply would meet demand. When that happened buyers might be expected to react to the prices being charged. General Motors couldn't roll the clock back to 1942, but it could cut costs to the bone by eliminating unnecessarily costly complexity in its product lines.

A more interesting question is why Cadillac had an essentially new design at all in 1950. It has been suggested by numerous observers that Cadillac did it deliberately in order to, in effect, "spend" its luxury market competitors into oblivion with an extravagant level of product development that they could not match. This theory, which meshes well with the American obsession with conspiracies, hardly seems consistent with the well-documented, cost-cutting attitude then prevalent within General Motors, nor does it seem consistent with the actual situation in the luxury field. When the 1950 Cadillacs were being developed, Imperial offered little threat. Clearly Packard, which had yet to develop its first truly new postwar body, was in no position to match Cadillac

1950 Series Sixty-Two convertible.

dollar-for-dollar in product spending, but Packard no longer posed much of a realistic threat, either. Ford, on the other hand, was the major competitive challenge across the board and was spending money like a drunken sailor (and, like a drunken sailor, often too much and none-too-wisely).

The essentially new Cadillacs bodies announced in 1948, 1950, 1954, 1957, and 1959, were met with a succession of Lincoln generations dating from 1949, 1952, 1956, 1958, and 1961. Moreover, unlike Cadillac which (with the lone exception of the Eldorado Broughams) shared General Motors bodies with other divisions consistently, Lincoln body shells were only intermittently shared with other Ford product lines. This had the effect of substantially increasing the development costs at Lincoln per se. In engineering, Cadillac developed its new V8 for 1949, but Lincoln introduced no less than three new engines in 1949, 1952, and 1958, while the 1956 engine was thoroughly reworked from the 1952 design. In addition, two entirely new Lincoln manufacturing facilities were built in this period, at Wayne in 1951 and at Wixom in 1957. The Continental Mark II was a far more ambitious program from a cost standpoint than that of the corresponding Eldorado Broughams (which were always semi-customs) and involved the construction of yet another new Lincoln manufacturing facility. Considering the evidence, it is certain that Ford outspent General Motors in the luxury field in the early years after the war, and, probably did so by a daunting margin. So, if Cadillac and General Motors really thought they could outspend their principal competition, they were soon disabused of that notion.

To the contrary, circumstantial evidence would suggest that the 1950 Cadillac program was a desperate rear-guard action undertaken to defend against perceived challenges from Lincoln and, to a lesser extent, Packard. During the latter part of the war, Frank Hershey and others at General Motors were assigned to develop a couple of highly advanced prototypes to demonstrate future design trends to General Motors management. These cars had the slab-sided, bathtub look to them that was a common feature of futuristic concept drawings of the era. They were rejected as too radical. General Motors would move at a more measured pace in keeping with existing design concepts. So, the 1948 C-body had been a logical styling development of the prewar design school pioneered at General Motors with Bill Mitchell's landmark first Sixty Special in 1938. All Cadillac styling—indeed, virtually all new General Motors products from 1940 to 1949—were conceptually derivative of that design. Moreover, Mitchell was head of the Cadillac design studio when the 1948s were done.

Much of the industry fell in line with General Motors, too, notably including Studebaker, Nash, and Packard (with the 1941 Clipper body). Ford,

where design was directed by E. T. Gregorie and under the influential pa-
tronage of Edsel Ford, resolutely marched to its own tune and built designs
that were preludes to the bathtub school. Chrysler and Hudson failed to emulate General Motors' success, mostly due to the hide-bound conservatism of
their managements, and to their lack of design sense, in general. When Hudson did move, though, it was with the force of a fault line that suddenly
wrenches itself free. The earthquake at Hudson resulted in the radically different "Step Down" series of bathtub cars introduced in 1948. The bathtub
Packards, reworked on the 1941 Clipper body, appeared concurrently, and the
similar 1949 Mercurys and Lincolns were introduced shortly thereafter. The
new Kaiser and Frazer cars also followed the same general design school.

The appearance of all of these radical postwar lines at virtually the same
time, and all enjoying major early success in the marketplace, must have been
deeply unsettling to those charged with charting General Motors' product
strategy. In particular, it was an open secret that the young Henry Ford II was
determined to reestablish Ford's position in the industry as the primary chal-
lenger to General Motors—and, apparently, intended to do so with bathtub
styling.

What is known is that 1948-series, C-bodied cars appeared in 1948 for both
Oldsmobile and Cadillac, and in 1949 for Buick. The Cadillac C-body limousine derivative scheduled for 1949, however, was scrubbed, and related B-body
cars for Olds and Buick never appeared, either. Instead, a new bathtub-like B-
body Buick Special was rushed into production for a mid-1949 launch, followed by the full range of similar B- and C-body Buicks and Cadillacs in 1950,
as well as the new B-Body Olds 98. The 1948-series General Motors C-body
had been in production less than two years at Olds and Cadillac, and a mere
nine months at Buick. This is all the more striking in light of internal General
Motors volume projections—upon which each division's share of the C-body's
tooling cost was based—that assigned 70 percent of the cost to Buick, compared to 16 percent for Olds and 14 percent for Cadillac. For Buick, those 1949
Supers and Roadmasters were expensive, indeed. Worse, Buick was allowed to
languish for the better part of a year without its volume Special series, while,
Cadillac was compelled to make do with the venerable prewar Seventy-Five for
yet another year.

In light of all the foregoing, it seems probable that the 1950 restyles at Olds,
Buick, and Cadillac were the result of a crash program to bring their styling in
line with what was perceived to be a sudden shift in design in the industry, in
general, and at Ford, in particular. The small General Motors A-body, shared
by Chevy, Pontiac, and Olds, appeared as planned in 1949 looking very much

like the 1948 C-body, but it, too, was scheduled for replacement in 1950 or 1951. It was only due to the Korean War that the A-body replacement did not appear until 1953, by which time Olds had shifted all of its models to the more contemporary B-body.

Toward the end of the 1950 model run, there was a major change in the top slots at the division. In July, Don Ahrens was rewarded for his decade-and-a-half of remarkable work building Cadillac sales with a promotion to general manager, while James M. Roche was named to Ahrens' old job. At the end of August, Ed Cole moved on and Charles F. Arnold was named chief engineer. Bill Mitchell had been succeeded at the Cadillac design studio by Joseph Schemansky the previous year, and Schemansky, in turn, would be followed by Edward Glowacke in 1951. The entire guard was changing, with well-deserved promotions the order of the day. In time, out-going general manager Gordon, then Roche, and then Cole, would all become presidents of General Motors in succession over over a span of 16 years. Roche would eventually become chairman, as well. Mitchell, for his part, would one day head the entire General Motors Design Staff, while Harry Barr would go on to be General Motors' top engineer. To say that the Cadillac team in this era was high-powered would be a massive understatement.

The 1951 model year was clouded somewhat by the Korean War, then at its peak. It was an uncertain period with memories of the radical dislocations of the early 1940s still fresh. Nor was it just paranoia. The Government was meddling in the car business again, with price controls and restrictive materi-

1951 Series Sixty-One sedan.

als allocations. Although not so onerous as in the years immediately preceding and following World War II, there were constant rumors of a cessation of civilian car production. Nothing came of it in the end, but it made for nervous times in Detroit. The auto industry was, once again, producing military hardware. In Cadillac's case, defense production consisted of tanks produced in General Motors' Cleveland tank plant.

Despite the dislocations caused by the war, Cadillac production soared to another record: a total of 110,340 cars were built during the model run and Cadillac registrations approached 2 percent of the industry total. This, in turn, sparked a serious debate at the highest levels within General Motors regarding the wisdom of letting Cadillac production pass the century mark. The concern was that the appeal of a Cadillac was, to a certain extent, dependent upon its rarity. Let them become too common, so the thinking went, and the appeal would diminish. In the end, it was decided to let Cadillac production follow a natural course. Nevertheless, the division followed a deliberate policy throughout the next couple of decades of keeping supply slightly below demand in order to insure that Cadillacs would never become too easy to buy. This program, whatever else its merits, guaranteed fat margins for Cadillac dealers until the oil shocks of the mid-1970s.

Probably as a consequence of the aforementioned concerns, the Sixty-One —the most affordable Cadillac line—was discontinued in mid-year. Only 4,700 were built in 1951. Across the board, Cadillacs featured larger bumper guards, which now jutted provocatively from heavy chrome bars, as well as

1951 Coupe de Ville.

1951 Seventy-Five.

modestly reworked trim details such as the new grilles below the head lamps. It was a minor facelift, to be sure. Inside, oil and battery gauges were replaced with warning lights.

Chrysler managed to scoop Cadillac in an embarrassing way in 1951 that sent General Motors engineers rushing to their drawing boards. Chrysler announced power steering for its Chrysler and Imperial lines. Ironically, General Motors had actually patented power steering in the early 1930s, but never put it into production because the depressed production levels at the time would not justify the investment. After the war, when demand was soaring, power steering was not needed to sell cars. If it had not been for Chrysler, it is hard to say how long it would have taken General Motors to get around to building it. The boys over in Highland Park, showing unusual initiative for them in this era, waited patiently for the General Motors patents to run out, then moved quickly to put power steering into production in 1951. General Motors was suddenly in a position where it had to play catch up with an important innovation it had invented—literally. Such is the car business. Power steering appeared on Cadillacs in 1952, and, by 1953, most other General Motors divisions had it, too.

If Cadillac was resting on its laurel wreath in 1951, the competition was not. At Packard and Chrysler new cars abounded. The first true postwar Packard was announced, featuring styling that was contemporary and abandoned the bathtub look that had quickly grown old in the marketplace. In fact, with its high fender line, the new Packard was arguably a more advanced design than the corresponding Cadillac. But, while pleasant, the new design was also very plain, and the product was still powered by the superannuated Packard straight eight engine in a market that was switching with a vengeance to high compression V8s. Worse, the Packard senior line was reduced to just one model, the 400 sedan. It was nicely trimmed and well-built, as befitted a Packard, but hardly enough to attract much attention all by itself. In mid-year, good-looking hardtop coupe and convertible models were added, and while these are often thought of by modern enthusiasts as luxury cars, they were designed and priced to compete with the comparable Buick Roadmasters. Packard was still targeting its resources at the medium-priced field.

The restyled 1951 Imperial offered a dramatically expanded range consisting of sedan, hardtop, convertible, seven-passenger sedan, and limousine models. At least on paper, it was the most competitive range of luxury cars Cadillac had confronted since before the war. Moreover, the new Imperial boasted Chrysler's technically advanced, hemispherical-combustion-chamber V8—the fabled Hemi—as well as power steering. Fortunately for Cadillac, the Imperial was also saddled with a couple of crippling shortcomings: the dowdy 1949 Chrysler styling that a mild facelift was powerless to transform, and the absence of an automatic transmission. This latter lapse should not be underestimated. A fully-automatic transmission was considered by most buyers to be absolutely essential in a luxury car by 1951, and its absence was a body blow to any serious hopes Chrysler had of making real headway with its new Imperial.

With all of Cadillac's potential luxury market competition offering threats of varying ambitiousness, it is useful to consider the situation that confronted players in the luxury field. Building a first-class car was not enough; it was necessary to sell it to someone and there were four basic target groups: 1) existing customers; 2) customers graduating up from less expensive brands sold by the same company; 3) customers graduating up from less expensive brands sold by other companies; and 4) customers "captured" from other luxury brands. Indeed, these categories are still valid today.

Of the four categories, the first is the Mother Lode. An old axiom in the marketing profession is that "a customer is yours to lose," i.e., once someone is buying your product or service, he or she is going to tend to continue to do so until given a compelling reason to change buying habits. For a car maker, mining the lode of existing customers is the easiest and most cost-effective way to sell new cars. Cadillac, with by far the largest customer base in the luxury field, was the big winner year-in and year-out in this category. Packard's decision to vacate the field—and thereby turn its customers loose—was the major marketing blunder in the luxury field in the 1930s and 1940s, but Ford did much the same thing on a smaller scale when it phased out its big K-Series Lincolns. Most of these Packard and Lincoln customers were eagerly snapped up by Cadillac. In truth, most had no place else to go, but they belonged to Cadillac by 1951.

The second category—customers graduating up from less expensive brands sold by the same company—is also potentially lucrative. Just as car buyers tend to develop loyalty to a particular brand, they also tend to develop loyalty to particular companies (and used to do so in the 1940s and 1950s much more so than they do today). Alfred Sloan built General Motors largely on this strategy. General Motors offered a full range of cars spanning the price spectrum so that customers could move up or down the scale, as desire or financial circumstance dictated, while still remaining in the General Motors fold. When they outgrew Olds or Buick, they could walk down the street to the Cadillac dealer—or perhaps across the showroom floor, for Cadillac was often dualed with Olds in those days—and still be a General Motors customer. Cadillac benefited mightily from this dynamic. Packard, of course, was severely restricted in this, as it had only a small presence in the medium-price field and none at all at the lower end of the spectrum. Ford and Chrysler, which did have well-developed product lines in the low- and mid-ranges, cultivated thousands of customers for Cadillac in the 1930s and 1940s.

The third category—customers graduating up from less-expensive brands sold by other companies—was one in which Cadillac had considerable success for many years due to the failure of Ford and Chrysler to develop credible luxury products and, thus, exploit the second category. The postwar decisions to develop the Lincoln and Imperial were at least, in part, an effort to stop the customer drain to Cadillac and General Motors at the top end of the scale by developing credible luxury car alternatives for loyal Ford and Chrysler customers.

The fourth category—customers "captured" from other luxury brands—was also one in which Cadillac had enjoyed considerable success at the expense of Packard and Lincoln, as the effectiveness of those two luxury brands disintegrated beginning in the mid-1930s. The revitalized Imperial, Lincoln, and Packard lines had little chance of stealing significant numbers of customers away from Cadillac unless Cadillac stumbled, and, to an objective observer, the prospects of that in 1951 appeared problematical, at best. It is difficult to believe that Chrysler seriously regarded the Imperial as a conquest vehicle. On the other hand, Jim Nance, Packard's new president, had great hopes of exploiting the residual strength of the Packard name to wean some former Packard buyers back, while Ford had clearly entertained expectations of conquest when the 1949-series Lincolns were announced. Ford's hopes, however, had soon been dashed. This was the final year for the first postwar Lincoln that was supposed to give Cadillac a fright, but succeeded mostly in panicking Ford executives by its failure to meet the ambitious (and probably unrealistic) goals set for it. By 1951, Ford engineers had sorted out the mechanical problems and the Lincoln had settled into being a pleasant, if uninspired, competitor, but Ford executives were counting the days and hours until they could be rid of it.

So, Cadillac still held a commanding position among luxury cars in 1951. It was the only make that offered a combination of contemporary styling and contemporary engineering. That was, however, soon to change.

Cadillac celebrated its Fiftieth Anniversary in 1952 with the smallest model range in nearly that long a time. Only seven models were listed in the catalog: the Sixty-Two sedan, coupe, Coup de Ville, and convertible; the Sixty Special sedan; and, at the top, a pair of Fleetwood Seventy-Fives.

Moreover, as minor as the product changes had been in 1951, they were even less cosmic in 1952. The war had dragged on into its third year, restricting the availability of chrome, copper, white sidewall tires, and cars in general. The "Korean War chrome" on 1952 cars has been a bane to old car enthusiasts for years. It is almost unheard-of to find a 1952 car with decent brightwork, although Cadillac seems to have gotten priority on what materials were available at GM.

Gold crests, in the wrap-around below the head lamps, signified the Golden Anniversary, while the tail pipes were routed through the rear bumper for the first time. Power steering, as noted above, was offered for the first time, as was the Autronic Eye automatic headlamp dimmer. Hydra-Matic was made standard equipment on all models except the Seventy-Fives.

The big news in the luxury field—and the most serious competitive chal-

1952 Series Sixty-Two sedan.

Top, 1952 Sixty Special; *bottom*, 1952 Series Sixty-Two convertible.

lenge Cadillac had faced since the 1930s—was launched by Lincoln with the
introduction of its entirely new 1952 models. Ford may have stumbled the first
time out with its 1949-series Lincolns, but the 1952 models showed they had
learned a thing or two from the experience.

The heart of the new Lincoln was its fully contemporary high-compression,
overhead-valve V8, but the hard work had not stopped there. Lincoln pioneered ball-joints for front suspensions and, in general, the Lincoln chassis was
splendidly engineered for handling and performance. Just how good a performer the 1952-series Lincolns were was demonstrated when Lincolns won the
next three Mexican Road Races in a row, leaving Chrysler Hemis and Cadillacs, alike, in the same cloud of dust. Lincoln had also dropped its medium-
priced lines, preferring to concentrate on the luxury field. In that, it scored
substantial gains. Lincoln's production of luxury-grade cars soared 72 percent
for the year, and the 27,271 cars built began to look like a potentially serious
threat to the 90,259 cars that Cadillac turned out.

The foregoing notwithstanding, it should be noted that the new Lincoln had its limitations, too. It was significantly smaller than the Cadillac, and this was a serious drawback in a market that was moving toward bigger cars—especially at the top-end. Its styling was also considered rather plain by most observers, and nearly all magazine road test reviewers in 1952 deplored the rather tepid power available from the new V8. The horsepower was duly increased for 1953, but the size and general styling were more difficult to modify and continued to restrain Lincoln sales to a degree.

Cadillac entered the 1953 model year officially in January, 1953, with the same model assortment offered in 1952. With the Korean War at last nearing its tortuous conclusion, sales throughout the industry soared, and Cadillac sold a lot of cars. In fact, it was the second best year on record, with a final production total of 109,651.

Cadillac claimed the highest horsepower ever used in an American production car: 210 horsepower. As these were the years of the prestige wars between Cadillac, Lincoln, Chrysler (and, to a lesser extent, Packard), however, just how reliable the quoted horsepower figures were is a matter of conjecture. Great strides in engineering were being made within the advertising departments of all luxury brand competitors in this era. The important thing was to

1953 Series Sixty-Two sedan.

claim impressive figures, and, if they were based on little more than the fevered imagination of a copy writer, no one seemed inclined to object.

The 1953 Cadillac models nevertheless did contain a number of changes, some of them of genuine significance. On the styling front, and in anticipation of the all-new 1954 models waiting in the wings, a little freshening was all that was offered. Imposing "dagmar" bumper guards projected from above the bumper. The name, common among designers (though never used for public consumption), was a droll reference to a buxom television starlet of the period whose main talent was her remarkable resemblance to the protuberances that now adorned the front ends of the new Cadillacs. Parking lights appeared under the headlights again, and the rear windows were of a one-piece design, the traditional mullions having been abandoned at last. The Sixty Specials continued to bear eight vertical louvers on the rear fender, but had wider rocker moldings.

Air conditioning was again officially available as an accessory, the first time since before the war that it had been listed. The new system was a significant improvement, though, in that it was no longer a full-time system. At the driver's option, the compressor could be turned off by a switch on the instrument

1953 Sixty Special.

panel. The air conditioning unit was, however, still located in the trunk, where it used up valuable storage space and made servicing difficult. For those reasons, it would eventually be moved to its now-familiar position under the hood.[2]

The big news this year, however, was the mid-year introduction of the Eldorado convertible. Loosely sharing a semi-custom convertible body with the Buick Skylark, the Eldorado featured a radical wraparound windshield, cut-down "sports car" doors, upgraded leather and cloth upholstery, wire wheels, and a semi-concealed top which lowered into a special fiberglass boot. The Eldorado's base price was a fairly astonishing (for the time) $7,750. At that tab, a grand total of 532 were sold that first model year.

The Eldorado was yet another tactical effort in the heating up luxury car war. That a hotter war was in the offing was obvious from the rumblings heard in 1953. Ford, it was rumored, was planning a return of the Continental in order to do battle with Cadillac at the top end of the segment in which the Eldorado was neatly positioned, as if in anticipation. Packard announced a limited-edition Caribbean convertible to match, and also added a couple of customs to the catalog—a formal sedan and a stretched sedan, available in both seven-passenger sedan and limousines configurations. It was produced

1953 LeMans show car with General Manager Donald Ahrens (at the wheel) and James Roche (standing).

President Eisenhower rides in his Inaugural parade in a 1953 Eldorado.

by Henney, the old-line professional car builder that had long been building Packard-based hearses and ambulances. Chrysler exhibited a series of "dream cars" that hinted at an end to stodgy styling—although the 1953 Imperials were as dowdy as ever despite some mid-run freshening—and, in mid-year, finally got an honest-to-gosh fully-automatic transmission. In that, the roles of Cadillac and Imperial were very nearly reversed.

In August, a catastrophic fire at the Hydra-Matic plant in Livonia, Michigan, resulted in a few minutes time in some $80 million in damage, the loss of several lives, and, quite significantly from Cadillac's perspective, the only source of Hydra-Matic transmissions for Pontiac, Oldsmobile, and Cadillac cars. The only saving grace was that the disaster occurred toward the end of the 1953 model run, for it happened during a reduced car production schedule and prior to a brief period when the lines would be shut down for the new model changeover. Nevertheless, all three divisions involved ran out of Hydra-Matic stocks. Cadillac and Olds quickly converted to the Buick Dynaflow transmission, while Pontiac switched to Chevy's Power-glide. One of the genuine crash programs in the history of the auto industry was undertaken by General Motors to rebuild Hydra-Matic. A new plant, new equipment, and new supplies all had to be put in place in record time, and the first Hydra-Matic unit from the new facility (the former Kaiser-Frazer factory at Willow Run) was produced in October—less than 90 days from the fire. It was nip-and-tuck, but Pontiac, Olds, and Cadillac all had supplies in time for the start-up of 1954 production.

While the functional end of the Korean War in 1953 temporarily helped spur production for most manufacturers, easy times in the industry were clearly over. This was because the unnatural seller's market, which had prevailed for a variety of reasons since 1945, finally and irrevocably ended. It had looked as if the traditional buyer's market would reassert its presence in 1950 as postwar production finally rose to meet demand, but the Korean War prompted Government production restrictions (intentional and otherwise) that halted the process for a time. The long-expected shift came in the spring of 1953, and its effects were sudden and brutal. So long as shortages lasted, all manufacturers benefited—even those building products that were seriously deficient for reasons of engineering, styling, or quality, or that were using weak dealer networks. It did not seem to matter. Only the very weakest (such as Kaiser) failed to sell large numbers of cars in the early 1950s. When the market suddenly became saturated, however, several nameplates all but vanished from the sales charts. Kaiser, Hudson, and Packard went into free-fall. Among the Big Three, Chrysler's inherent weaknesses finally came home to roost with a vengeance, with sales and market share collapsing overnight by nearly 40 percent.

CHAPTER FOUR

1954 Series Sixty-Two sedan.

Fending Off the Competition:
1954–58

FOR CADILLAC, the timing could not have been better. The 1954 Cadillac bodies were entirely new and sported fresh, dramatic styling that made a remarkable contrast to the dowdy Packards and Imperials for sale down the street. Even Lincoln, now in the third year of its successful 1952-series cars, began to look a bit dated. Worse, the Achilles' heel of the Lincoln—the fact that its body was significantly smaller than that of the Cadillac—was exacerbated by the new Cadillac bodies, for which the wheelbase was extended three inches to 129 on standard models, and up to 133 inches on the Sixty Special.

The new Cadillac bodies featured the familiar dagmars, now swept into inverted gull-wing bumpers. The grille was restyled, with a finer mesh egg crate texture. All Cadillac models featured the wraparound windshield pioneered by the Eldorado in 1953, and had an air intake positioned at the top of the cowl. The quoted horsepower rating was increased to 230, while the model range remained unchanged. Unlike in 1953, the Eldorado used the standard Cadillac convertible body, presumably to save costs, although with the usual amount of special trim inside and out. The decision to forego a semi-custom body resulted in a significant lowering of the asking price to a more affordable—and perhaps more plausible—$5,738. Sales quadrupled in response.

The year proved to be the fourth best in Cadillac history. Sales were down slightly due to a mild recession, but still exceeded the 100,000 mark for only the second time. An impressive 96,680 cars were built during the actual 1954 model run, of which 2,150 were Eldorados.

Cadillac sales and production soared again in 1955. Indeed, it was a banner year for the industry as a whole—the best on record up to that time—and Cadillac did its level best to contribute to the statistics. In that, the division outdid itself, for Cadillac sales and production reached all-time record levels up to that time. Production for the year totaled 140,777 cars.

The cars themselves were little changed, with minor trim alterations being about the extent of it. A one-piece side trim molding swept up into the rear fender, replacing 1954's two-piece molding. A new grille featured wider spacing

Top, 1954 Eldorado; *bottom,* 1954 Series Sixty-Two convertible.

of the mesh, and parking lights were moved back under the headlights. The Sixty Special sported twelve vertical simulated louvers on the rear fenders.

The major design news was the Eldorado. Although still based on the standard convertible body, it featured exclusive rear quarter panels of a radically finned design. Also featured was a special high-output V8 rated at 270 horsepower (20 horsepower more than the standard Cadillacs). The base price rose to $6,286, but production nearly doubled to 3,950.

The 1953 Eldorado, while a semi-custom, had looked little different from the standard line and, thus, it was no doubt difficult for many potential buyers to justify the price differential. The 1954 model, while far more favorably priced, was not nearly so appealing in its styling; the standard Sixty-Two convertible was arguably a better looking car. In 1955, Cadillac designers finally hit upon a design which permitted affordable manufacturing costs, but still gave the Eldorado a sufficiently unique appeal to attract a significant clientele. The Eldorado also became, to a certain extent, a stalking horse for Cadillac design in this era. The 1955 rear fins, for example, would reappear, in modified form, on the standard 1958 Cadillac range. There were other examples of this foreshadowing to come with future Eldorados.

Luxury market competition intensified in 1955. Chrysler announced an entirely new range of products from the Plymouth to the Imperial, which was now officially a distinct nameplate and no longer a top-end Chrysler. Only two Imperial models were offered, but the design was fresh, the mechanicals were fully contemporary, and it showed that Chrysler was capable of mounting a serious challenge as soon as it felt like committing the cash required to do so.

1954 Seventy-Five.

Packard mounted an even more impressive effort to reestablish its presence in the luxury field, although it was an effort made with limited funds and proved to be Packard's swan song. Since Packard could not afford a new body, the 1951 shell (dubbed "old high pockets" by Packard insiders because of its unfashionably high beltline) was pressed into service. Extremely skillful restyling by a youthful Dick Teague—later to head the American Motors design staff—turned new fenders, and an imaginative use of exterior trim, into a car that looked entirely fresh and exciting. Beautiful new interior trim rounded out the styling package, while a couple of major technical advances added to the cause. Packard finally got a modern V8, and also boasted torsion-bar suspension, front and rear. Financial problems at Henney precluded editions of the long wheelbase models Packard had offered in 1953 and 1954, but the 1955 Packard senior line was the most ambitious of the postwar period.

The Packard torsion bar suspension was interesting for a couple of reasons. First, it was interesting as a technical exercise that, in the view of most contemporary observers, raised Packard to the forefront of ride and handling in the luxury field. For the first time in years, Packard had a major selling point that Cadillac (and the other luxury makes) did not. Second, it was widely thought in the industry that following the revolution in engine technology represented by the high compression, overhead-valve V8, suspension advances would be next. This proved to be wrong, but enormous attention was paid to suspension technology in this era and Packard was suddenly in the lead.

As it turned out, none of the competitive efforts had much negative impact on Cadillac sales in 1955. While Chrysler enjoyed great success with most of its 1955 line, the Imperial was too modest an effort to make much headway. Packard, on the other hand, seemed to be moving ahead for a time until quality control problems turned the public against it. Jim Nance, Packard's president, had shifted the entire assembly operation to a new plant just as 1955 production was starting. It seemed that the old Packard management had invested as little in the manufacturing facility as they had in product development. Nance decided that the answer was to remove Packard from its traditional home on West Grand Boulevard (ironically, just down the street from today's state-of-the art Cadillac plant at Hamtramck) to a new facility. It was ill-considered. Largely as a consequence, Nance fought quality control disasters for most of the 1955 model year and, by the time he got them fixed, the new Packards were fatally tainted in the minds of luxury car buyers.

Packard did, however, influence Cadillac in the area of suspension development. It was partly in response to the scare General Motors felt with regard to the wave of new suspension technology begun by Packard in 1955 that air-

Top, 1955 Sixty Special; *bottom*, 1955 Coupe de Ville.

suspension was developed for introduction on Cadillac and other General Motors lines in 1958.

The entire Cadillac range received a pleasant facelift for 1956, a model run that was destined to be the final one for the 1954-series body shell, but the big news was the four-door hardtop Sedan de Ville. This model had been predicted by the Orleans show car of 1953, but was not the first such body type in the industry. Olds and Buick had rushed their own versions to market in 1955. The four-door hardtop Sedan de Ville was a handsome car, though, and contributed to what turned out to be another record year for the division.

Other than the four-door hardtop, styling changes on view when the new Cadillac models were announced in October, 1955, were more apparent than real. Up front, there was a new, finer grille mesh. "Cadillac" in script was featured on the grille itself, while the parking lights were relocated yet again, this time resting in the bumper. Small vertical bars surrounded the headlights. These cars were very close carry-overs to the 1955 range, but the designers did their work well and they seemed much fresher than they really were.

There were two new models for 1956: the four-door hardtop Sedan de Ville and a new two-door hardtop in the Eldorado line, called the Seville.[1] The Seville featured a grained Vicodec (vinyl) roof. The convertible was now known as the Biarritz. Both Eldorados continued the essential styling of the 1955 model with trim updates, and special gold finish grilles and wheels were a new option. The horsepower rating rose to 305, a figure resolutely pegged at 20 more than the lesser Cadillacs. Along with the rest of the Cadillac line, El-

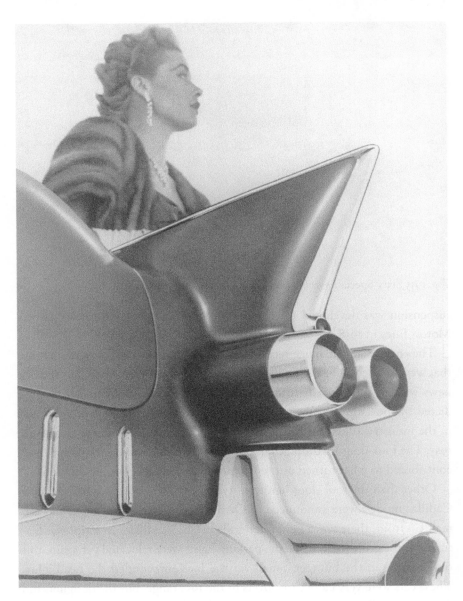

1955 Eldorado.

dorado sales were markedly up, thanks at least in part to the Seville. Both models carried a base price of $6,556.

Cadillac production, in general, reached a dizzying 154,577 units in 1956, of which 6,050 were Eldorados. Most of the Eldorados (3,900) were Sevilles, demonstrating the shrewdness of that decision, while 2,150 were Biarritz convertibles.

The 1956 model year, on the other hand, proved to be the end of the line for Packard. While the name would stagger on for another two years attached to glorified Studebakers, the true Packards died at the conclusion of the 1956 run. It was a sad end to a noble competitor and it is hard to believe there were not a few moist eyes even on Clark Street.

If Packard was leaving the field, Lincoln was back in the fray armed with two entirely new products: the all-new standard Lincoln range and the long-awaited Continental Mark II, which was technically a separate nameplate, although few in the industry wasted much effort making the distinction. The Mark II turned out to be a marvelous dud. A very handsome car, and highly sought-after today by collectors, it was simply over-priced at $10,000 and never came close to meeting Ford Motor Company's ambitious hopes that it would turn into something akin to an American Rolls-Royce. Ford wanted it to be seen as a motor car whose price and appeal was so far removed from ordinary mortal competitors that it would exist in a rarefied world of its own. In practice, the only rarefied world in which the Mark II existed was the empty showrooms in which it languished and the effort was abandoned after two disappointing model years.

1955 Eldorado.

The standard Lincoln range, ironically, did much better. It was, by consensus, the best-looking luxury car of 1956—only excepting the Mark II. Sales soared and it began to look as if Lincoln might at last be poised to offer a serious challenge to Cadillac's supremacy.

If so, there would be a new Cadillac general manager to deal with it. Don Ahrens retired at the end of 1956 and was succeeded by Jim Roche. As was the case with his predecessor, Roche's top-notch work as the division's sales manager had richly earned him a promotion to the general manager's office.

Top, 1956 Coupe de Ville interior; *bottom*, 1956 Sedan de Ville.

The entire Cadillac line was new for 1957 as a result of the second major body change since 1950. Of note was the introduction of the tubular X-frame without side rails and a center section of various lengths to allow different wheelbases. This increased structural rigidity and allowed for lower body lines, but it also left passengers woefully exposed in side-impact collisions. It was eventually augmented with a box-type perimeter frame for precisely this important reason.

The styling of the standard Cadillac range was both fresh and controversial. The most obvious feature was the pair of reverse-canted fins that some people liked a lot (this writer for one) and other people did not like at all. A double-finned hood ornament replaced the venerable goddess. Bumper guards, i.e., dagmars, were slightly raised and were rubber tipped, giving a rather suggestive look to them that was probably unintentional. The grille was composed of a fine mesh pattern, with the dual parking lights inset in the front bumper. Wheelbases were lengthened slightly on the standard chassis to 129.5 inches, while the Sixty Special remained at 133 inches.

As in 1956, the Eldorado range without question was the most exciting in the history of the series. The cars were dramatically different from other Cadillacs—even from each other within the Eldorado line. The "standard" Eldorado Biarritz and Seville sported their own rear end sheetmetal featuring bulbous rear quarter panels. Atop them sat tapered fins that seemed too delicate for the rear end mass, but the overall effect was still effective and pleasing. The new Eldorado Brougham, on the other hand, was not only the highest priced regular production Cadillac ever at $13,074, and the last model ever built by Fleetwood. These Eldorados are rightly placed among the most sought-after collectibles of the entire postwar era.

The Brougham, which was (to no one's surprise) positioned to compete with Lincoln's Continental Mark II, had its genesis with a four-door hardtop show car, the Orleans, in 1953. From this mostly-stock Cadillac evolved the radical (but handsome) Park Avenue of 1954. The Park Avenue, in turn, developed into the Eldorado Brougham show car of 1956, which was frankly billed as a pre-production car. This was most likely an attempt to take some of the wind out of Lincoln's sails, for when the Brougham finally appeared it was quite different in appearance (although carrying most of the show car's styling themes in a general way). Entirely custom-built in the Fleetwood plant in Detroit, the Brougham boasted a host of special features: quad headlights, brushed stainless steel roof, air-suspension, low profile ties, special engine, the highest level of interior trim (including genuine mouton carpeting), and about a zillion electric gizmos for the convenience and/or amusement of owner

1957 Coupe de Ville.

and passengers—and the likely bewilderment of mechanics at Cadillac deal-erships across the land.

Although the quoted base price was $13,074, it seems highly probable that most Broughams—like most Continentals—were sold for considerably less. In both cases, the quotation was an example of inverse price competition. Cadillac "won" the price war, but it is difficult to believe that either company made a dime off their glorious white elephants. An almost invisible 400 Broughams were built in 1957, and Lincoln recorded a comparable 444 Con-tinental Mark IIs. Lincoln pulled the plug on the Mark II at the end of the 1957 model run, while Cadillac kicked the Brougham "upstairs"—out of sight and out of mind—to Pininfarina in Italy for 1959.

Although the Biarritz and Seville confined their unique styling to the stan-dard Cadillac body and chassis, they were considerably more flamboyant than the other Cadillacs and undoubtedly far easier (and cheaper) to manufacture. As before, they were finished with upgraded materials through, including the Vicodec roof on the Seville, as in 1956. The common base price was $7,286. A total of 2,100 Seville coupes and 1,800 Biarritz convertibles were built.

Cadillac production dipped in 1957 to 146,841, still making it the second best year in the division's history up to that time, while market penetration for the calendar year actually increased slightly, from 2.23 percent of all cars sold to 2.36 percent. This showed remarkable strength in the face of the major challenges the division faced in 1957.

Meanwhile, Lincoln continued its successful 1956 models with some modi-fications inspired by the Futura show car.[2] The most controversial of these were the outward-canted rear fins, which many observers thought ruined the clean 1956 design. Regardless, Lincoln sales held fairly steady at around 41,000 cars, which was a heady rate of production by Lincoln standards. But, an even more troubling challenge was mounted by Chrysler.

If Cadillac management had never taken the Imperial very seriously, it could be forgiven. In truth, the Imperial had never amounted to much. In 1957, however, that suddenly changed. The entire Chrysler range, from Plymouth to Imperial, was stunningly new. Virgil Exner's design teams had grabbed the lead in American automotive design in an advance that caught General Motors totally unawares. The clean lines, lowered beltlines, and aggressive wedge shapes coming from Highland Park made everything General Motors had in production or on the drawing boards look antiquated by comparison. Curiously, the best examples of the new Exner styling were at the extremes of the price spectrum, i.e., the Plymouth and the Imperial. Worse, from Cadillac's perspective, the Imperial now boasted a full range of cars in three lines positioned to compete head-to-head with most of Cadillac's standard models; only the Eldorados and Seventy-Fives were left without direct challenge, and there was no telling when that might appear. Imperial sales tripled in 1957, and Imperial and Lincoln be-

1957 Eldorado Bourgham.

tween them were suddenly selling at a rate around half that of Cadillac. This still left Cadillac solidly in the lead, of course, but at around half the edge it had enjoyed as recently as 1951. Moreover, with an entirely new range of Lincolns in the wings for 1958, even that lead suddenly seemed tenuous. Something akin to panic swept over General Motors in 1957, and this would have a dramatic effect on the design of the 1959 Cadillacs.

In the meantime, the 1958 Cadillacs were mildly revised versions of the successful 1957 cars throughout the range. On standard models, the trim was juggled around, the grille mesh was modified in a way that predicted the design in the works for 1959, and the fins were canted the other way. "Quad" headlamps were featured on all models, and the Sixty Special had a wide aluminum panel on the lower rear fender that was similar to 1957, but that now included skirted fenders. Other than that, the differences were relatively minor; the big styling news would come in 1959. Changes were even less apparent with the Eldorado Seville and Biarritz, and were confined mostly to the front-end styling shared with lesser Cadillacs and rear grilles. At the top, the Brougham was virtually unchanged.

The model range was also unchanged from 1957, with the exception of the new Sixty-Two extended deck model. Built on the hardtop sedan body, this model featured an 8.5-inch extension of the rear deck. Basically, it was a Sixty-Two hardtop sedan built on the Sixty Special body. It was only offered for the 1958 model year.

1957 Seventy-Five sedan.

One of the engineering "advances" in 1958 had actually appeared in 1957. This was air-suspension, which was standard on the Eldorado Brougham and now optional on other Cadillac models, and it was among the worst ideas to ever escape from Detroit. The General Motors' system quickly joined the auto industry's pantheon of totally unreliable and discredited devices alongside the 1923 "copper-cooled" air-cooled Chevrolet engine and the 1942 Lincoln Liquimatic semi-automatic transmission. The idea worked well in commercial applications (buses, trucks, etc.), but was cheapened so severely for passenger car application that it was virtually useless for any length of time. The seals leaked, the air bags cracked, and, in general, it was a thoroughly unsatisfactory application of a basically sound idea.

Cadillac production dropped significantly due to the second Eisenhower-era recession. The final total stood at 121,778, although market share increased significantly to 2.63 percent of all cars sold during the calendar year. The most notable change was the sudden decline in Eldorado sales. A drop of 57 percent in Eldorado Seville and Biarritz production was recorded, of which 855 were coupes, 815 were convertibles. Brougham production, which had never been high to begin with, dropped to 304 units.

Meanwhile, the big news in the luxury market in 1958 was the collapse of the competitive challenges mounted by Imperial and Lincoln. This was as significant a development as the decision of Packard management not to mount a full-scale effort in the luxury market after the end of World War II. In the

1957 Eldorado Seville.

Top, 1958 Eldorado Brougham; *bottom*, 1958 Sixty-Special.

case of Imperial and Lincoln, however, the critical missing ingredient was not will, but execution.

The entire 1957 Chrysler corporate product range had been immensely appealing and did remarkably well for a time. Unfortunately, Chrysler manufacturing standards faltered under the pressure, resulting was a shocking loss of quality. Fit and finish was a nightmare; thousands of owners were angered by new cars that rattled, squeaked, and rusted. To be sure, the Imperial, which was always more carefully built than lesser Chrysler products, probably suffered less than its corporate stable mates, but the difference was only relative. The simple truth is that Chrysler sold hundreds of thousands of cars in all price ranges in 1957 that should never have been shipped and paid a frightening price in terms of damage to its traditional reputation for engineering excellence. Thousands of first-time Imperial buyers vowed never to repeat their error, and uncounted thousands more were dissuaded by word-of-mouth reports from those who did. Unquestionably, the Imperial brand—and, arguably, Chrysler Corporation as a whole—never recovered from the fiasco. This was certainly good news for Cadillac, though, and there was more to come with the arrival of the 1958 Lincolns and Continentals.

Ford was determined that 1958 would at last be the breakthrough year for Lincoln. The ill-starred Continental Mark II was transformed into a new upper-end series of the Lincoln line, comparable to the Sixty Special but available in an array of body types. The design was entirely new and prepared by a team headed by John Najjar. Najjar decided that Imperial was into aggressive wedge shapes, Cadillac was into roundness with fins, and so staked out Lincoln's new direction as aggressive angularity. The new Lincolns and Continentals were immense, made even more so by the decision to build them on the world's largest unibodies. This latter decision was made very late in the game due to the need to augment four-seater Thunderbird production at Ford's projected Wixom, Michigan, plant, and resulted in Lincolns that were (at least initially) quality control disasters rivaling the Imperials of the previous year. Worse, and unlike the Imperials, the new Lincolns and Continentals were generally regarded as ponderous and ugly by luxury car buyers. In combination, the design and quality lapses prompted a slide in Lincoln sales of near catastrophic proportions, particularly as word-of-mouth from early owners spread the quality story (or lack thereof).

CHAPTER FIVE

1954 Eldorado Biarritz.

Cadillac Hits Its Stride: 1959–64

CADILLAC REACHED a zenith of sorts in 1959. The Cadillac styling studio, in the opinion of many, had gone completely berserk and the resulting finned wonders were almost cartoon caricatures of themselves. Indeed, that is one of the reasons for their enduring popularity (especially in Europe, where they are regarded as being quintessentially American, an idea that ought to give us all pause). It is helpful—indeed, with many cars of the late-1950s, it is absolutely necessary—to try to imagine them within the context of their own times. The 1959 Cadillacs didn't look quite so garish in 1959. In fact, they were rather successful, and the story behind their creation is the stuff of a sensational, made-for-television movie. The only element missing is the steamy sex—and if anecdotes about General Motors' design studio in Harley Earl's time are to be believed, that lapse is probably due only to the fact that such things were not deemed fit to record for posterity.

Long before the 1958 models made it to dealer showrooms, a genuine crisis erupted. As has been alluded to earlier, it happened just as the all-new 1957 Cadillacs were being announced to the public. To understand the situation, a little history is in order.

Most industry observers and enthusiasts alike are accustomed to thinking of Chrysler as the number three auto producer, and generally a poor third, at that. It was not always so. From the mid-1930s to the early 1950s, Chrysler enjoyed the second slot, having passed Ford when that company began to fall out of touch with developments in the industry in the latter years of the reign of Henry Ford I. After World War II, the roles were reversed when Henry Ford II set out to regain Ford's position as chief rival to General Motors.

At the same time, Chrysler, under the arch-conservative leadership of K. T. Keller, was falling farther and farther out of touch. Chrysler, with one of the best engineering staffs in the world, stoutly resisted the increasingly popular automatic transmission, regarding it as a passing fad. Worse, the new 1949 Chrysler models, as has been noted, were so painfully conservative in their styling that it became increasingly harder to move them even in the seller's market of the early postwar period. These were two major reasons the Imperial, for example, failed to gain many adherents in this period. It was soon became more and more obvious to Chrysler management that fresh blood was needed in the design area. Virgil Exner was specifically hired to provide it.

Following a stint at General Motors (he was largely responsible for the design of the 1938 Pontiacs), Exner joined Studebaker's design staff where he created the striking 1947 Studebakers, the first all-new postwar cars from any major manufacturer.[1] After losing its second place status to Ford in the early 1950s, Chrysler management borrowed hundreds of millions of dollars and gave Exner the green light for a crash program to design an entirely new line of Chrysler products for 1955. When these cars were a big success, Chrysler

1959 Sixty Special.

1959 four-window Sedan de Ville.

management told Exner to do it again for 1957 and, this time, Exner pulled out all the stops.

Looking back, the Chrysler "Forward Look" cars of 1957 may well prove to have been the post-World War II high watermark of Chrysler Corporation as an auto producer. Although remembered today mostly for their gargantuan tail fins, they were breathtaking in their clean lines, flat hoods that rested far below the fender lines, expanded use of glass for light, airy greenhouses (including the industry's first use of curved side window glass on some models), dramatic wedge shapes, and, on most lines, restrained use of chrome trim. The Plymouth slogan that year—"Suddenly It's 1960!"—was more than just the product of an over-eager copy writer's imagination; it was palpably true. From the Plymouth all the way up the price scale to the Imperial, Chrysler was suddenly setting the design standard for the industry. The people over at Ford weren't excessively bothered by this; they had an impressive new Ford for 1957, and dramatic new Edsel and Lincoln models in the works for 1958 (both of which turned out to be flops, although they couldn't have known it in 1956). General Motors designers—especially the younger designers such as Cadillac's Charles M. "Chuck" Jordan—were stunned.

It was Jordan, in fact, who first stumbled onto what Chrysler was up to. Today, the trade and enthusiast magazines regularly publish "spy photos" of new models months or years before they go into production. It was not like that in the 1950s. The auto makers kept a much tighter leash on their new products. At new model announcement time, it was common practice to go so far as to ship the new cars to dealers hidden under tarpaulins, lest anyone get an unauthorized peak. Jordan was in the habit of driving by a Chrysler plant located near the new General Motors Technical Center (where the Design Staff had been relocated) to gather what chance intelligence he could from freshly-built cars awaiting shipment in the holding yard. That was where he spied the first 1957 Plymouths and reported his discovery to his Design Staff colleagues.

The Olds, Buick, and Cadillac B- and C-bodies were new for 1957, the new Chevy and Pontiac A-body was already locked-up for 1958, and they all looked like your grandmother's corset next to their direct competitors from the Chrysler stable. General Motors designers were beside themselves, and General Motors management joined the panic when Ford pulled ahead of Chevy in sales as the new model selling season opened in the fall of 1956. Ford hadn't made that kind of a breakthrough since 1935. Something had to be done—and fast.

So, shortly after the New York Auto Show in December, 1956, the corporate decision was made that all General Motors brands should have essentially new cars for 1959. At first, largely at the behest of strong-willed design chief Harley Earl, a crash effort was mandated to restyle the 1957–58 bodies. Earl, who loved the bulky, chrome-laden barges that had become the signature of the corporation's design efforts in the 1950s, was due to retire at the end of 1958 after three decades in charge, but he still called the shots. He insisted that the current bodies could be worked-up to do just fine, then left for Europe.

At this point, General Motors' designers began to openly rebel. Convinced that the current bodies were unsalvageable, designers in all General Motors studios, in a spontaneous uprising, began working on their own entirely new bodies across the board for 1959. Thus, for several incredible months, two sets of 1959 cars were under development: the revised 1958 models insisted upon by Earl, and the all-new cars the designers were beginning on their own.

The designers were not without support in their rebellion. William Mitchell, the former Cadillac design chief who was slated to assume Earl's job, had been chomping at the bit for a chance to invigorate the corporation's design efforts. He was joined in this view by General Motors' president Harlow Curtice and by the divisional general managers. There was a growing sense that the corporation was falling behind in design compared to other companies in the industry. In fact, Paul Gillan, head of the Pontiac design studio was certain that Earl was sent to Europe to get him out of the way! Ed Glowacke, chief designer in the Cadillac studio since 1951, recalled that Earl didn't feel at all comfortable with the transition that was taking place:

> We all had our new designs going, either on one side of a clay model or as a
> separate model. Every studio had something new going. There was just so
> much concern over these cars [from Chrysler], and what we'd been doing was
> so old that everybody rebelled. So, when Mr. Earl came back from Europe,
> the studios were saying, in effect, "this is how we want to do it."[2]

Glowacke moved on up in the Design Staff heirarchy in August, 1957, and was replaced by his assistant, Chuck Jordan. For his part, Jordan credits Bill Mitchell as the main force behind the new direction at Design Staff:

> He [Mitchell] had that vision. It wasn't Harley Earl who had the vision, and it wasn't Harlow Curtice . . . Mitchell was the guy who made the '59s happen. When Harley Earl wasn't around, Mitchell was in all the studios, and he was it![3]

In any case, on April 4, 1957, after four months of turmoil, Earl caved in. Entirely new bodies would be developed across the board for 1959. The official decision came down directly from the Engineering Policy Committee whose chairman was the General Motors vice-president in charge of engineering, Charlie Chayne, and included General Motors' president, executive vice-presidents, the group executive in charge of the car divisions, the group executive in charge of body and Buick-Olds-Pontiac (B-O-P) assembly plants, and the vice-presidents in charge of styling, research, and sales. It was not a casual decision, particularly in light of the 17 months remaining until the planned 1959 new model announcement, barely half the time usually allotted for development of a new body. In order to make it work at all, an unprecedented degree of standardization across General Motors lines would be required.

Rooflines were interchangeable in all General Motors car lines from Chevy through Cadillac, as were front doors, which were standardized across the board from the Buick design, since that was the one completed first. In fact, there was really only a single, shared B-body in 1959, as the corporation contracted from three body shells to one, although Buick (Electra only) and Cadillac did rate a unique, six-window four-door hardtop roofline. Even the Cadillac Sixty Special used the new, 130-inch wheelbase B-body from 1959 until the next generation of full-size bodies was tooled for 1965. Cadillac insisted on calling it a C-body, regardless. The Eldorado Seville and Biarritz were stuck with stock Cadillac sheetmetal, as well, making this the first time the Eldorado had done so since 1954. On the other hand, the 1959 program actually resulted in an increase in the number of Cadillac models from 12 to 13 as both four- and six-window four-door hardtops were offered on the Sixty-Two and the Sedan de Ville, while the extended-deck Sixty-Two sedan was deleted, there being no longer an extended-deck body available.

Ironies abound in the saga of the 1959 General Motors design program. As has been noted, Chrysler, which had started the whole panic, all but destroyed its once enviable reputation for engineering excellence due to the unspeakably shoddy quality of many of the cars actually built. Chrysler soared to better than 18 percent in market share in 1957, only to tumble to barely 11 percent by

1959—a more dreadful level of penetration than the one that had prompted the Forward Look campaign in the first place. General Motors, which turned itself inside out attempting to match the Wonder Cars from Highland Park, saw most of its 1959 nameplates languish—including Chevrolet for whom the battle was primarily waged.

Even Ford, which hadn't been bothered by Chrysler, went into a panic when it learned Chevy was mounting a crash program to produce all-new 1959 models. In response, Ford scrapped its already finished 1960 designs, which were to have been based on its highly successful 1957-59 body, and pulled the new 1961 design a year forward in a crash program reminiscent of General Motors' experience with its 1959s—only to see the "old" 1959 Fords outsell the new Chevy and the new 1960 Fords falter in the market, at the same time engendering the same sort of problems Chrysler had faced due to poor quality resulting from their rushed production.

So, to sum up the situation, of the five 1959 General Motors car lines, Chevy and Buick—the corporation's cash cows—were outright disasters; Oldsmobile (the most conservatively styled of the five) had a so-so year; and only Pontiac and Cadillac were solidly successful. The 1959 Pontiac "Wide Tracks" set a successful design theme for that brand that continues to this day, while the 1959 Cadillacs have come to be regarded as among the most memorable cars of the era, for good or for ill.

It may come as a surprise to readers that designers tend to regard the 1959 Cadillacs with a considerable degree of affection. This is understandable as

1959 Seventy-Five.

1959 Eldorado Bourgham.

they were closer to "pure" designs than most produced by Detroit. Jordan himself noted of the design, "Harley Earl told me, 'you just pile it on and I'll take it off.' The trouble was, he never took anything off!"[4] Although the most notable feature of the design was its exaggerated tail fins, designers point out the unbroken sweep of the beltline from front to rear, and the relatively restrained use of brightwork (the Sixty Special being an exception to this). One important technical feature that almost got lost in the furor surrounding the 1959 program was that this was the first year for acrylic lacquer paint, a General Motors mainstay for many years to come.

As if defying the laws of gravity, the Eldorado Brougham still had its own body. Moreover, it was completely new. It was not, however, being built by Fleetwood, or even in the United States. For one reason or another, the Brougham was now being built in Italy by Pininfarina. It has long been assumed that the numbers involved failed to justify taking up plant space in Detroit, although the cachet of a European coachbuilder's name might have been a lure. Given the crash nature of the 1959 General Motors body program, though, farming the Brougham out may have been the only way it got built at all. The standard Cadillac chassis was shipped to Italy, fitted with its body and shipped home for the final touches by Fleetwood. Practically everything in the Cadillac arsenal was standard, including the increasingly notorious air-suspension (also standard on the Seville and Biarritz). The most interesting thing about this model is the way in which it previewed standard Cadillac styling for the coming 1960 model year. In fact, one interesting feature would not appear until 1961: the almost-non-wraparound windshield. The base price was listed at $13,075.

Cadillac production rose along with that of the rest of the industry as the nation came out of the 1958 recession. A total of 142,272 were built. Eldorado production rose slightly to 2,295, of which 975 were Sevilles, and 1,320 were

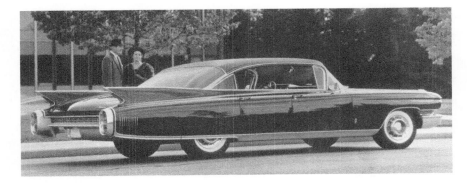

Top, 1960 Sixty Special; *bottom*, 1960 Eldorado Brougham.

Biarritz convertibles. Brougham production, however, sagged to an almost invisible 99.

The 1960 Cadillac models were toned-down versions of those offered in 1959. The compact car boom was on; big and flashy were no longer "in." Even the luxury rigs felt they had to trim their sails a bit. Still, after the Herculean exertions of 1959, no one at General Motors had much energy left when the 1960 models came around. In fact, the big news at the division was the arrival of a new general manager. Roche moved on up in the GM ranks (eventually to become president, then chairman), and was replaced by Harold G. Warner.

The 1960 Cadillac model line-up was unchanged and just about the only development of note was with the low-volume Eldorado Brougham. It was revised again for 1960, although it remained essentially similar to the previous model. It was still being bodied by Pininfarina and it still previewed the next year's design with its very-1961 styling. A mere 101 Broughams were built. Overall Cadillac production remained flat, while market share remained virtually unchanged from 1959.

In sum, this is the way matters stood on Clark Street as the 1960 model year drew to a close: Its traditional top competitor, Packard, had withdrawn from the luxury market after 1956 and ceased entirely by the end of 1958, while its two insurgent competitors, Imperial and Lincoln, had both largely self-destructed. While Imperial and Lincoln would no doubt remain in the market for the foreseeable future, it would be a long time before either would likely be in a position to mount a serious challenge to Cadillac's luxury market supremacy. The years since peacetime production resumed in 1945 had seen Cadillac's luxury market position repeatedly attacked by all of its competitors. Through it all, Cadillac fought the tough fight and emerged the same way it had entered—the unchallenged leader of the luxury field.

There appeared to be no one left to question Cadillac's supremacy. If a challenge came, it seemed as if it would have to come from somewhere else and assume, perhaps, some unforeseen form.

The important news of the eara was the first great compact car boom. The Rambler had set the industry on its ear in 1958 when it suddenly caught fire with the public and, in 1960, the Big Three had weighed in with compacts of their own. By 1961, every General Motors division, save Cadillac, offered a compact. If Cadillac management was not anxious to enter the fray, it was at least observing the trend with a wary eye. In fact, there was considerable speculation within the industry regarding just how far the public's new-found fancy for smaller cars would extend.

Not that the Big Three were seriously worried about little American Motors, of course, or much less about those funny little foreign cars that were suddenly so popular. It was probably a passing fad, just like the tail fins and

1960 six-window Sedan de Ville.

1961 Sixty Special.

three-tone paint schemes of the 1950s. Cadillac was content to build on its hard-won recent successes. Thus, the division began to settle into a comfortable maturity, and even felt sufficiently secure to begin paring back its product offerings.

The first model to go was the Eldorado Brougham. Like the V16 in the 1930s, it had been a magnificent irrelevance designed to counter a threat that never really materialized and, like the V16, continued on through a second generation long after the potential danger had passed. It is harder to understand why the Eldorado Seville also got the ax in 1961; it had been selling nearly as well as the Biarritz convertible model that was retained.

The 1961 Cadillacs, completely redesigned on the 1959 body shell, were well received. The economy was down a bit in 1961, though, and so were Cadillac sales. Final production stood at 138,379. If sales dipped, they did so throughout the industry, and the division was actually able to register a small increase in its market share.

The new grille was convex to form a sharp "V," while the dual headlights were set in the grille, which is to say much lower than before. In back, the dual taillights appeared side-by-side, rather than stacked as in 1960. In general, the 1961 models were the cleanest in years in terms of their restrained use of brightwork. Even the Sixty Special was relatively unadorned, and looked even more handsome than it had for a long time with its new limousine-type roofline. Only the Eldorado Biarritz retained a hint of its former gaudiness.

There were few exertions of a technical nature for 1961. In fact, the most notable engineering news was the deletion of air-suspension, a demise regretted by few. Wheelbases were shortened on standard Cadillac models to 129.5 inches, down half-an-inch from 1960, overall length was reduced by a full three inches, and a short-deck Town Sedan was added to the de Ville series at mid-year. The Town Sedan was identical to the six-window Sedan de Ville except for a seven-inch reduction in length at the rear which, a special brochure assured prospective buyers, was "just enough to answer special metropolitan motoring problems without altering the beauty of the car's silhouette." A total of 3,756 Town Sedans were built during the 1961 model run.

In addition to the public's sudden fancy for smaller cars, an unspoken influence on Cadillac's sudden interest in down-sizing may have been the 1961

Top, 1961 Seventy-Five interior; *bottom*, 1961 Coupe de Ville.

Lincoln Continental, which was built on a 123-inch wheelbase and was nearly three inches shorter than even the Town Sedan. The small size of the Lincoln was, to a certain extent, an illusion. True, it was shorter than the Town Sedan, but, owing to the particularly inefficient application of unibody construction it used, it was actually around 250 pounds heavier. Still, it looked smaller and more efficient, and that seemed to fit the temper of the times. No one on Clark Street could be certain that the boys over in Dearborn weren't onto something. In fact, the boys over in Dearborn were flailing in great confusion. But, it was inspired flailing. In their desperation, they came up with a new car that finally set Lincoln on a course from which it might one day mount a challenge for luxury market leadership.

After almost disappearing from the sales charts with their ill-fated 1958-series Lincolns and Continentals, Ford Motor Company executives began to despair of ever developing a car that could compete against Cadillac. While dropping the Lincoln was never seriously considered, funding was drastically cut. A more serious problem was what to do for the new car that would be needed in 1961. Most Lincoln-Mercury executives were of the view that one of Lincoln's problems had been the radical changes from model-to-model. Unlike Cadillac, which seemed to convey an air of comfortable familiarity through its

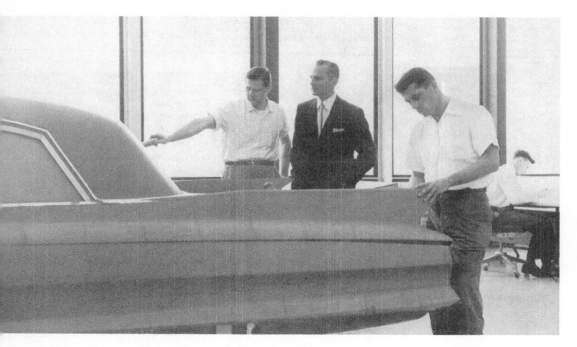

1961 Seventy-Five clay model in the design studio circa 1959. Charles Jordan, the chief designer, is the one in the middle.

1961 Eldorado Biarritz.

products even when they were completely revised, every new Lincoln since the war had been so different in nearly every way from its predecessors that it might have been built by a different company. The result was terminal confusion among luxury car buyers as to what exactly a Lincoln was—confusion, it must be said, that was shared in the halls of Dearborn. It was better, the line of thinking went, to settle on a single design theme—even an unsatisfying one—and stick with it for a period of years in order to build up consumer recognition, than to be charging all over the map trying this and then that. Accordingly, a 1961 Lincoln was developed following 1958 design themes.

Then, one day, Robert McNamara, at the time president of Ford, chanced to be walking through the design studios when he spied a full-size Thunderbird clay that had been worked up by Elwood Engel along Mark II design themes. McNamara was impressed and directed Engel to stretch it enough to make room for four doors. This Engel did and the result was so pleasing that the mock-up became, virtually without further alteration, the 1961 Lincoln Continental, a car not only firmly rooted in Lincoln design tradition, but nearly revolutionary in its untrimmed, slab-sided good looks. It was widely regarded as not merely the most appealing car of 1961, but one destined to be a future classic. Only its relatively high price (it was positioned against the Sixty Special) and limited model range (due to Lincoln's reduced budget, four-door and four-door convertible models were the only ones offered) kept it from doing better in the market. It set an enduring design direction for Lincoln and also influenced design throughout the industry for decades to come. Ironically, executives at GM and Chrysler were perhaps even quicker to appreciate the potential threat presented by the 1961 Lincoln Continental than were the people who created it—as events in the next several years would demonstrate.

The Cadillac range was granted a mild facelift for the 1962 model year. A new, blunter grille was the most prominent element in the revised design. It came with a prominent horizontal bar and Cadillac in script in the lower right corner. Rectangular parking/directional signal lights were positioned below the headlights in the fenders. Cornering lights were similarly located, while vertical, multi-action taillights in the rear bumper housed driving lights, stop lights, turn signals, and back-up lights. The heater/defroster unit was made standard.

Sales recovered along with the quickening pace in the industry, reaching a new high. Big cars, in particular, seemed to be coming back into vogue. That, and increased national prosperity, saw Cadillac production rise dramatically and set a new all-time record: 160,840 units.

The model line-up was essentially carried over, with a couple of noteworthy exceptions. The number of short-deck sedans was doubled to two. The new Series Sixty-Two Town Sedan was not to be confused with the 1961 Town Sedan, which had been a de Ville and was renamed the Park Avenue Sedan de Ville. The reason for this game of musical nomenclature went unrecorded, but Cadillac management's faith in—or fears regarding—the popularity of smaller luxury cars was misplaced. Only 2,600 of each model was built.

After the overall success of the 1962 range, it came as a mild surprise when the 1963 Cadillacs were seemingly all-new. In fact, they were heavily revised versions of the successful 1961-62 models, and represented the second and final major restyling on the 1959 body shell. The styling showed a keen appreciation of the influence of the 1961 Lincoln, the car that had, as has been noted, almost single-handedly introduced the "less is more" school of design in Detroit. Suddenly, less trim or even—will wonders never cease?—less size was acceptable in a luxury car. The new Cadillacs were hardly small. In fact,

1963 four-window Sedan de Ville.

1963 Sixty Special.

they were slightly longer than the models they replaced, but they were much cleaner than in years past, with tasteful sculpturing supplanting more garish sculpturing and acres of chrome. In particular, the progressively disappearing fins excited much favorable comment at the time.

As with the trimmer tail fins, the 1963 styling seemed a simpler version of themes that Cadillac had been using for several years. The Sixty Special and El-dorado showed the greatest Lincoln influence with their smooth, unadorned flanks, yet they all looked like Cadillacs. The grille was quite similar to that used in 1962, while the headlamps were raised flush with the fender overhang. The cowl louvers had a finer mesh, and were divided by a bright metal piece at the hood crease. In common with the Sixty Special, real wood was offered in the Eldorado Biarritz interior and a short, wood-trimmed console was included with the bucket seat option. It made for a handsome interior.

The model line-up was similar to that offered in 1962, the exception being the Series Sixty-Two Town Sedan, which was dropped. There was major engineering news in the engine compartment. While displacement and horsepower remained unchanged, the 1963 V8 was one inch lower, four inches narrower and one-and-a-quarter inches shorter. The 1962 engine had been entirely cast iron, the new engine used aluminum accessory drives to save about 82 pounds. Production rose to a new record level in 1963, as 163,174 units were built.

The 1964 Cadillac line was only slightly revised from 1963. The bolder and slightly "Veed" horizontal bar across the grille was mirrored in a similar reworking of the rear end. The Biarritz designation was no longer used, but the Eldorado featured the handsome new Fleetwood rocker panel moldings and, to emphasize its sporty flavor, open wheel cut-outs in the rear. The interiors, especially with the optional console and bucket seats, were especially impressive. Other than that, there were no major changes to the styling or to the model line-up except the deletion of the Park Avenue Sedan de Ville, the last of the short-deck Cadillacs.

The biggest news for 1964 was on the engineering front. The displacement

Top, 1963 Series Sixty-Two convertible; *bottom,* 1964 Eldorado.

of the engine was upped to 429 cubic inches, and Turbo-Hydra-Matic transmission was offered for the first time. Turbo-Hydra-Matic was a three-speed torque converter-type automatic that replaced the original Hydra-Matic that, in some form, had been around since 1941. On the accessories front, the Twilight Sentinel was offered for the first time. This option, which was to become immensely popular with Cadillac owners, turned the head and taillights on at dusk and off in daylight, while a delayed action feature allowed the lights to stay on briefly for illumination after the car was parked.

Cadillac production rose to a new record for the third time in three years. A total of 165,959 cars were built, yet it was not enough to maintain Cadillac's market share, which fell below two percent of industry sales for the first time in years. There were a couple of prime reasons for this: Lincoln and Imperial.

Once given up for dead, Cadillac's two domestic competitors showed some signs of life in 1964. As influential as the 1961 Lincoln had been on Cadillac design, Chrysler had paid it the ultimate compliment: Elwood Engel, the designer, was hired away to work his magic on the Imperial. The result appeared in dealer showrooms at the start of the 1964 model year and attracted considerable interest. Sales, too, rose smartly for a time, then settled back into the doldrums as the freshness wore off. Before that happened, though, a few customers were snatched away from Cadillac.

Meanwhile, Ford, which had legitimized smaller luxury cars, finally decided the only way to get Lincoln sales off dead center was to make them bigger. The Continental was, therefore, reworked into a somewhat larger package for 1964, although the general 1961 styling was maintained. Lincoln sales rose smartly and, unlike the case with Imperial, stayed at the new, higher level.[5]

To be sure, Lincoln and Imperial between them sold fewer than a third as many cars as Cadillac in 1964, but it was the best performance for both in years and chipped away a little at the massive lead Cadillac had built up in the luxury field. In Lincoln's case, the brand was at last attaining a level of public respect long sought for it by Ford. If this was not yet fully reflected in the sales figures, it at least offered cause for hope in Dearborn—and cause for concern on Clark Street.

CHAPTER SIX

1966 Eldorado.

At the Apex:
1965–70

THE 1965 CADILLAC LINE announced in September, 1964, featured the first completely redesigned body shell since 1959. The styling—done under the direction of Stanley Parker, who had succeeded Chuck Jordan as chief of the Cadillac studio at about the time the 1965s were starting their design development—was more angular than in previous years. This was still more evidence of the pervasive influence of the 1961-series Lincoln Continental, but very pleasing and very much in keeping with long-established Cadillac design themes.[1]

The major news, and what attracted the most comment at the time, was the apparent abandonment of the tail fins. Actually, the development was more apparent than real; the fins were still there although they now receded to a level even with the beltline. In time, they would rise again. The 1965 grille was in the typical Cadillac mold, but with stacked dual headlights.[2] Fenders and doors were more slab-sided than ever, and all models used the bare minimum of bright trim. In back, the subtle tail fins ended abruptly in vertical taillights of a general design that would become a Cadillac standard in coming years.

There was major engineering news this year with the new bodies, and with the abandonment of the X-frame in favor of a perimeter frame which not only afforded much needed side-impact protection for passengers, but also allowed the repositioning of the engine six-inches forward. In addition, while the model line-up was the same as in 1964, the Sixty Special and Eldorado returned to a separate, stretched wheelbase after six years of sharing the smaller chassis.

Cadillac broke with long-standing tradition and eliminated numeric series designations. Thus, the Sixty-Two was divided into two series, the Calais and the DeVille. The only series that still carried the old number for public consumption was the Seventy-Five, but it was formally considered part of the new Fleetwood series, along with the Sixty Special and the Eldorado (which had been listed in the Sixty-Two range heretofore). For reasons that remain unclear, the old Seventy-Fives themselves were carried over unaltered from 1964. With six years between major body changes, it is hard to believe they did not have time to engineer a new long wheelbase chassis. Meanwhile, the number of models listed remained as before, although the previous complement of four- and six-window four-door hardtops on the standard chassis was supplanted with four-window, four-door hardtops and pillared four-door sedans. This was also the year the Brougham was first listed as a Sixty Special option; it consisted mainly of a vinyl roof. As in recent years, the Eldorado re-

1965 Sixty Special.

Top, 1965 Eldorado; *bottom,* 1965 Series Seventy-Five limousine.

mained little more than a high-grade trim option, but a singularly handsome one on the lengthier Fleetwood chassis. The Eldorado got its rear fender skirts back, which served to emphasize the new length, and bucket seats were a no-cost option. "Tamo" wood was featured on Fleetwood models.[3]

Cadillac production soared to undreamed-of levels in 1965 with a final total of 181,435 units seeing the light of day. It was hard to remember that as recently as 1950 there was heated debate within Cadillac as to whether production should be permitted to exceed 100,000 units per year. Eldorado production increased, as well, to 2,125, the most Eldorado convertibles built in any one year since 1955. Cadillac market share rose back above 2 percent, too, so the 1965 range must be considered a major success in virtually every respect.

There were a number of important personnel changes at the division in this era. Charles Arnold, who had been chief engineer for a decade-and-a-

1967 Coupe de Ville.

half, retired in February, 1965. He was succeeded by Carl A. Rasmussen. The following year, general manager Harold Warner retired and was followed by Kenneth N. Scott. After serving for five months, Scott was named to head Fisher Body. His replacement was Calvin J. Werner.

The 1966 Cadillacs were only slightly revised from previous range, although the long-awaited announcement of the Seventy-Five models on the new body shell was welcome news to buyers in that small, but important, market segment. Styling revisions, while confined to details, were especially felicitous. Essentially, the hard edges of the 1965 design were rounded and softened a bit. The 1966 range is regarded by many Cadillac enthusiasts as being particularly desirable. There was little to report in engineering developments, however. The model line-up, too, was virtually unchanged, although the Brougham was moved off the Fleetwood Sixty Special option list and was now a separate model in the Fleetwood Series.

This was to be the final year of the rear-wheel-drive Eldorado, the end of one era and the beginning of another. If the Eldorados of the 1961–66 period did not have the excitement of the earlier models, or the sporty appeal of the later models, they were, nevertheless, special automobiles. They were built to the very highest level of Cadillac standards in quality and luxury, which was arguably the best in the world at this time. They were fine cars and deserve more attention from collectors than they have received to date. No doubt their time will come.

If Cadillac was between major product developments in 1966, its main competitor had important news to report. Lincoln announced the first major restyling on its trend-setting 1961 design. The new models were lengthened and given a more sculptured look, while remaining within the general design

parameters laid down five year earlier. A significant departure was the introduction of a two-door hardtop, a body type that Lincoln market research had
indicated was sorely needed if the nameplate was to expand its customer base.
Lincoln sales rose only modestly in response, but the overall Lincoln achievement thus far into the decade was significant. Lincoln had come from a paltry
10 percent of the luxury cars market in 1960 to nearly 19 percent in six years.
The 1966 market share was Lincoln's best since 1956 and, in absolute numbers
of cars built, the best year in the marque's history. Cadillac was still selling
three-out-of-four luxury cars manufactured in the United States, but Lincoln's
strength was growing.

Yet, Lincoln was not alone in setting a record in 1966. Cadillac produced
196,675 units. While its share of U.S.-built luxury cars fell marginally, its
share of total industry registrations was up for the second year in a row.

The full-sized 1967 Cadillacs were completely reskinned and restyled, although still based on the 1965 body shell. While maintaining Cadillac styling
themes, the new cars wore sheetmetal that was more heavily sculptured than

1967 Coupe de Ville.

had been seen in many years. The frontal design, in particular, was far more aggressive. The grille extended below the bumper to partially surround the license plate frame, while distinct fender hoods appeared above the headlights. Still, models and mechanicals remained virtually unchanged.

With the Eldorado, it was a completely different story—to say nothing of a completely different car. In fact, 1967 may be marked as the birth of the modern Eldorado. From 1954 to 1967, Eldorados had been flashy, trimmed-up versions of the full-size line (excepting the 1957–60 Broughams, of course). From 1967, they would assume a unique character and would be positioned as America's leading examples of what came to be known as "personal luxury" cars, a type that had been pioneered in as early as 1950 by the Muntz Jet and really hit the big time in 1958 with the four-seater Ford Thunderbird. Buick had followed in 1963 with its stunningly beautiful Riviera, and Oldsmobile had blazed new trails with its front-wheel-drive Toronado in 1966, but there still were no personal luxury cars from the ranks of the true luxury marques. All that changed with the 1967 introduction of the new Cadillac Eldorado.

Ironically, the Buick Riviera could very easily have been a Cadillac. This design was developed by General Motors design staff as an answer to the surprising popularity of the four-seater Thunderbird, then shopped around to the General Motors automotive divisions. All put in a pitch for it, with Buick winning the right to produce it. Actually, the competition was rigged to some extent. Harlow Curtice, who had made his career with Buick, was still General Motors' president, while Buick, suffering from its sales collapse of 1958–59, clearly needed a shot in the arm. By the mid-1960s, however, it was fast becoming imperative for Cadillac to get an entry of its own in this market, if only in self-defense. Too many potential Cadillac buyers were being lost not only to the Thunderbird, but to the Riviera, as well.

The 1967 Eldorado shared its basic body shell and drive train components (excluding the engine) with the Toronado, but there the similarity ended. The Eldorado's styling was entirely its own and proclaimed its Cadillac heritage in every visible way. Special Eldorado features included concealed headlights, full-length side windows that did away with the traditional vent panes, automatic level control, and variable ratio power steering. The doors were so long that special rear remote handles were offered for back seat passengers.

Cadillac production finally reached 200,00 units in 1967, and the 17,930 Eldorados built undoubtedly helped push sales upward toward that mark. Cadillac sales for the calendar year recorded the second-best share of overall registrations in the division's history, while its share of American-built luxury car sales topped 80 percent for the last time ever. Overall, the 1967 model year could rightly be regarded as the postwar high watermark of Cadillac as a luxury car producer.

If things were booming for Cadillac, that could not have been good news for Lincoln and Imperial. Lincoln sales fell sharply from 1966's strong pace, and the attention garnered for Cadillac by the new Eldorado undoubtedly contributed to that. This was Cadillac's year and the Eldorado was the most exciting event in the luxury market. This fact must have contributed also to the pallid showing of the all-new line of Imperials announced for 1967. These models shared the Chrysler body shell for the first time since 1959 and were, by any rational measurement, the best Imperials in years. Described in the 1967 Imperial brochure as "relentlessly thoughtful," the model range incorporated a host of ingenious features, including a "Mobile Director" option in which a small conference table unfolded from the front armrest, and a cabriolet vinyl roof that pioneered the type that was to become a popular standard in the luxury field in coming years. And, it did them no good at all. In 1966, Imperial had posted its worst luxury market penetration in a decade, and the completely redesigned 1967 models were barely able to match that. It was a dismal performance that must have been extremely disheartening for those charged with the Imperial's destiny.

Considering the level of success Cadillac had attained in 1967, it was not surprising that there was little design news to report the following year. The

1967 Coupe de Ville.

1968 Eldorado.

1968 Cadillacs were, across the board, only mildly facelifted. The big news was in engineering: the first completely redesigned V8 engine since Cadillac's landmark high compression, overhead-valve V8 of 1949. Although more powerful and quieter, this engine gained back the 80 pounds the previous engine lost. Its main features were the emission control air injection passages in cylinder head, cast Armasteel connecting rods, a metal temperature monitoring device (which afforded a sort of early-warning system for serious engine overheating), and an integral water crossover pipe with thermostatic passages.

On the styling front, a new grille on full-size models featured a finer mesh texture, while rear side marker lights were located in taillight bezels. One-piece molded interior door panels made their first appearance, while the Eldorado sported concealed windshield wipers, a development pioneered by Pontiac the previous year.[4] Parking lights were mounted on the leading edge of the front fenders, the taillights were larger, and there were other alterations in keeping with new government regulations.

The model line-up was reduced with the deletion of the Calais pillared four-door sedan, marking the early stages of an eventual phase-out of this low-end series. The Calais had accounted for 19 percent of Cadillac production as recently as 1965; by 1968 this was down to 8 percent and soon would virtually disappear. At less than $300 in savings for what was a significantly plainer automobile, there simply was not a sufficient price differential to lure many buyers into a Calais.

For the Eldorado, and for Cadillac in general, the big news was that Lincoln had decided to join the fray with a luxury personal car of its own: the Continental Mark III. The Mark III appeared in the spring of 1968 and was technically considered to have been an early 1969 model (and was serial numbered as such). In time, the Mark Lincolns would become the most popular Lincolns of all time, outselling the Eldorados in some years. True to form, Chrysler was a day late and a dollar short, never joining the battle until its reborn Imperial of 1981, and experiencing little luck even then.

Still, Cadillac posted another all-time record year in 1968, with some 230,003 cars built. It seemed ill-mannered to argue with apparent success.[5] Cadillac management clearly believed that the marque was on a roll in this era, and, in truth, there was little enough to challenge that viewpoint.

As had become routine, the full-size Cadillac line was restyled in 1969 fol-

1968 engine.

lowing the usual two-year cycle. As is in recent years, the restyling was done primarily to freshen the appearance of the line, not the introduced dramatic new design advances. The basic package had changed little since 1959, although there was a continuing program of refinements and improvements. The 1969 range was demonstrably superior to the Cadillacs of ten years before and, in fact, are regarded by many connoisseurs (together with the 1970 models) as the finest models of this era.[6] The most notable (and controversial) design development was the elimination of vent windows across the board. Cowl vent louvers were also eliminated, while directional signals/parking lights wrapped around fender edges and merged with cornering lights.[7]

Unlike the full-size bodies, the Eldorado shell was little changed. The Eldorado sported a new, fine mesh, non-notched grille with stationary headlights separate from the grille. Eldorados equipped with the optional vinyl roofed featured the new "halo" separation at the outer edge.

Cadillac production dipped a shade to 223,237 units overall in 1969. Cadillac's share of total industry registrations for the year, however, came close to matching the all-time high set in 1958. For 1970, Cadillac production rose to all-time record levels for the third year out of the previous four. A total of 238,745 cars were built. It was a fine welcome for George R. Elges, who had succeeded Calvin Werner as general manager in July, 1969, just as the 1970 models were due to enter production.

The full-sized 1970 Cadillacs were close in appearance to the 1969s, with only detail refinements to differentiate them. The Eldorado, again, was little

1969 Eldorado.

1970 Series Sixty-Two convertible.

changed in design. The big news was the mammoth new 8.2 liter (500 cubic inch) engine. This 400 horsepower monster was the largest engine available on a production car in America, or anywhere else for that matter. A power-operated sunroof was optional, the first time Cadillac had offered a sunroof option since the years immediately before World War II.

Cadillac's domestic competitors were active in this period, as well. Another all-new Imperial had been introduced for the 1969 model year and was continued over with detail modifications for 1970. Unfortunately, it incorporated the Chrysler "fuselage" design concept that proved to be unpopular with many buyers despite the advance in automotive design it represented. Chrysler bodies were wider at the middle (where shoulder and hip room were needed) and narrower top and bottom. This was a trend that would be followed by all manufacturers in coming years, but it did little to benefit Imperial sales, which were in a slow, and ultimately fatal, decline.

Lincoln, on the other hand, was gathering strength. The Mark III had proven itself to be a solid hit in the marketplace and came very close to matching Eldorado production in 1970. Meanwhile, the standard Lincolns were given their first completely new body since 1961. It resulted in the largest car since 1960 and brought Lincoln to rough parity with the full-size Cadillacs in size. Overall, nearly one-out-of-four luxury cars built in America in 1970 was a Lincoln and this was, by far, the best market penetration in Lincoln history.

CHAPTER SEVEN

This 1973 Eldorado paced the famed Indianapolis 500 race.

Trouble Brews:
1971–79

IN 1971, as if in acknowledgment of the fresh challenge it faced, every car Cadillac built was new. The designs had begun their evolution at about the time Stanley Wilen was named to head the Cadillac studio, replacing Stan Parker. The full-size models sported a much trimmer, more youthful appearance that made appealing use of the "fuselage" design concept first introduced by Chrysler in 1969. Unlike the Chrysler execution of the concept, however, the Cadillac (and General Motors) versions involved a relatively low beltline and an expanded use of glass in the greenhouse area. Ironically, in an odd switch in image, the Eldorados seemed less youthful and more substantial in appearance than their full-size stable mates.

The basic 1971 styling cues, aside front the fuselage body design, hearkened back to the 1969 models in the frontal design and all the way back to 1966 out back, where the taillight assemblies were once again sequestered in vertical chrome bumper ends, although without the chrome divider. A distinctive feature of the front were the headlights that were widely spaced in individual bezels. The Sixty Special Brougham featured a unique separation between front and rear doors that continued up into the roof via the "B" pillar. Basically, what Cadillac had done was put the stretch between the doors rather than in the rear door, as had been done on Sixty Special sedans since 1965. It was a highly original treatment, but worked well.

Eldorado styling was similar to the rest of the Cadillac range, but differed in numerous details; the headlights were not separated, and the taillights did have the vertical bar in the center. The Eldorados also featured a vertical side molding behind the doors that was reminiscent of a theme last used in 1954 (and in modified form on the 1957–58 Broughams). Public reaction to the new models was mixed, with the full-size line finding general favor, while the Eldorado did not.

The model line-up had some interesting additions and deletions. Gone were the pillared Sedan de Ville, the DeVille convertible, and the Fleetwood Sixty Special sedan. Added was an Eldorado convertible, the first since 1966. On balance, the line-up was reduced by two models to nine, the smallest number since 1955.

A UAW strike against General Motors at the beginning of the 1971 model

A pair of 1971 Cadillacs: *top*, Sedan de Ville; *bottom*, Eldorado convertible.

Top, 1972 Fleetwood Brougham; *bottom*, 1972 Seventy-Five limousine.

run held down production. The final total, 188,537, was the lowest since 1965. Still, market share for the calendar year was up substantially due to the popularity of the 1971 models and their 1972 successors that were introduced in September, 1971.

Cadillac—indeed, the entire luxury field—took a breather in 1972. At Cadillac, most of the effort (such as it was) was spent on refining the 1971 design, i.e., tightening up the bodies and so forth. Many of the 1971 full-size bodies from Fisher had been noticeably weak in terms of torsional rigidity and this, in turn, led to a host of customer complaints due to squeaks and rattles. The problem was not completely fixed until the 1973 model year.

There were few changes in either full-size Cadillac models or in the Eldorados. Bumpers featured protective rubber strips, while the parking lights on full-size models were moved out of the bumper to a position between headlights. It was Cadillac's Fiftieth Anniversary and, in celebration of that, the Cadillac wreath and crest emblem appeared on the hood of the Fleetwoods, and on a small pedestal of the Eldorados. There was also a new two-piece boot for the Eldorado convertible and a mid-year Eldorado Cabriolet vinyl roof option.

With industry attention focused on meeting government mandated engineering changes, and considering that the cars were all new in 1971, it's no wonder that little happened to the line this year. Sales surged ahead, however, reaching an all-time high as industry sales cracked the ten million mark. A record total of 267,787 cars were built. Eldorado production also reached a record: 40,074.

Lincoln was having a good year, too, though. In fact, on the strength of the new Mark IV, Lincoln set a production record of 94,560 cars that was 50 percent greater than the preceding record. Mark IV production was up an astonishing 79 percent—to 45,969 units—and Lincoln now had the clear lead in a significant market segment for the first time ever. So, for Cadillac, its record year was tempered by the knowledge that an aggressive competitor was beginning to gain significant ground. For the first time in 15 years, the division was forced to contemplate the possibility of having to fight for sales leadership.

Still, meeting Government emissions and safety standards consumed most of the engineering energy at Cadillac when the 1973 models were being developed. The 1973 Cadillacs were only mildly revised in appearance, mostly due to the high-strength, energy absorbing bumpers mandated by the Gov-

1972 Eldorado coupe.

1973 Sedan de Ville.

ernment. On full-size models, this resulted in an attractive new beaver-tail rear end, but emissions regulations took a toll under the hood. Engines were hard to start and balky, and delivered the worst fuel economy in Cadillac's modern history.

The Cadillac range, now in its third model year, received a number of design refinements. Up front, an emphatically vertical grille appeared that was more in keeping with the developing fashion for pseudo-radiator-type designs. The new rear design with "beaver tail" slope as the rear deck flowed into the bumper, has been mentioned. Eldorado models received a facelift for 1973 that simplified some of the busyness of the 1971–72 designs. A pronounced egg crate grille adorned the front end, while the vertical side moldings were gone. An illuminated Cadillac crest on the rear fender formed the side marker light. The Cabriolet option continued.

The division got replacements in two of its top slots in January, 1973. The new general manager was Robert D. Lund, and the new chief engineer was Robert J. Templin. They arrived just in time to see Cadillac sales and production rise to yet another all-time high. A total of 304,839 Cadillacs were built during the 1973 model run. Eldorado production, 51,451, was also an all-time record. But, for Cadillac, and for the entire industry, the good times soon came crashing to a halt.

In the winter of 1973-74, the Arabs succeeded where Lincoln, Imperial, and Packard had failed: They stopped the steady rise in Cadillac sales. The Arab oil embargo hit the entire industry with a body blow that was felt with special severity in the high-priced field. Industry sales in the 1974 calendar year slumped by 3,000,000 units. Sales picked up dramatically after a few months, however, and overall production for the year was only down about 20 percent to 242,330.

Full-size Cadillac models were distinguished by a return to the egg crate design grille given to the Eldorado the previous year. The top surface of the rear bumper was lowered and the horizontal stop, backup, and taillights were located in a urethane body colored bezel. The Eldorado sported a new, fine

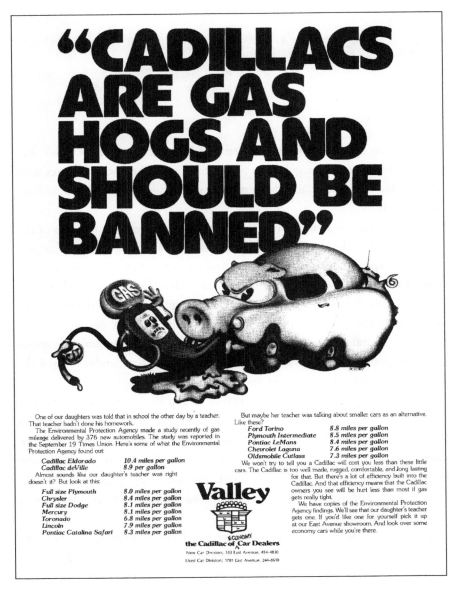

1973 Cadillac newspaper advertisement.

mesh grille and received the new bumpers, too, but the Cadillac crest side marker lamp was eliminated.

One of the more intriguing interior trim options offered on any Cadillac in modern times was the Fleetwood Talisman, listed in the catalog for both 1974 and 1975. It featured huge center console/arm rests front and rear—it was literally a four-passenger car—and all of it was garbed in the most garish crushed velour imaginable. Indeed it rather strained the imagination. Production figures are not known.

This was also the year of the notorious seat belt interlock system, in which the driver had to fasten the belt, insert the key, and engage the ignition in a set sequence before the car would start. If the driver failed, or used the incorrect sequence, the ignition was locked out and the whole sequence had to be repeated. This device raised such a cry of protest from American motorists that it became the only safety regulation ever to be rolled back by popular demand. The catalytic converter, which made its appearance the following year, caused no such uproar. Still, motorists who thought they could cheat with cheaper leaded gasoline soon discovered how poorly a car with a degraded catalytic element performed—and how expensive a replacement could be. (This is assuming their negligence didn't prompt the converter to catch fire and send the whole car up in smoke.)

Chrysler made one last stab at jump-starting its Imperial this year. The 1974 Imperial range was completely revised along with all full-size Chrysler products. Although it continued to share most of its exterior sheetmetal with lesser Chrysler offerings, the 1974 Imperial was a very appealing car in many ways. It attracted a considerable amount of attention until the Arabs stopped it dead in the water just as the product launch gathered steam. As a result, Imperial sales stalled yet again for the umpteenth and final time. From this point, they would go into a decline that would see the nameplate disappear by the time the 1976 Cadillacs arrived at dealer showrooms.

The major news from Cadillac in the 1975 model year was the appointment of another new general manager in November, 1974. Bob Lund, after less than two years on the job, moved over to the head office at Chevrolet. His replacement was Edward C. Kennard. Kennard's career had been in sales, and he moved up as general sales manager from Pontiac. He was destined to man the helm at Cadillac for nearly a decade and see the division through one of the most turbulent periods in its history.

The 1975 products represented another holding action for Cadillac. There was a new grille, as per usual practice, but the most distinctive design feature of the new models was the square head lamps in square bezels which wrapped around the fender to house the cornering lamps. These were standard on all models, including the Eldorados. The most striking feature of the new Eldorados, however, was the reversion to full-wheel cut-outs on the rear quarter panels.

While industry sales struggled, remaining at their lowest level since 1964, Cadillac production continued its post-embargo resurgence and reached 264,731 units. Eldorado production rose to 44,752 for the year, which was a good year, but not good enough to overtake the Lincoln Continental Mark IV, which seemed permanently dominant in this lucrative sub-segment.

Imperial production ceased at the close of the 1975 model run. Lincoln, on the other hand, boasted the first major facelift given its full-size models since

1974 Calais coupe and sedan.

1974 Eldorado coupe.

the last body change in 1970. It did not do much to change Lincoln's sales position with regard to Cadillac, though, but the boys over in Dearborn continued to sell about one out of every four luxury cars built in America.

On May 1, 1975, Cadillac introduced the "down-sized" Seville, and this was the really big news of the year for the division during the remainder of the 1975 run. It must be noted, though, that while the Sevilles were introduced and sold during the 1975 model year, they were given 1976 model serial number designations. Still, models built during the 1975 model run used 1975 colors and trims.

For a number of years, several foreign makes, most notably Mercedes-Benz, had been proving that Americans would pay real money for compact luxury cars. This fact had been ignored as long as humanly possible by Detroit, but the suddenly emergent energy crisis forced both Cadillac and Lincoln to come to terms with reality. Cadillac rushed its Seville to completion in the spring of 1975. Its reception was enthusiastic and Lincoln had no choice but to follow suit, although the comparably positioned Versailles would not appear until March, 1977.

The Seville was based on the General Motors NOVA (Nova, Omega, Ventura, Apollo) body shell. The 180 horsepower, 350 cubic inch V8 was sourced from Oldsmobile, although Cadillac engineers did considerable work revising it to meet Cadillac specifications. The engine aside, Cadillac had gone to extreme lengths to differentiate the Seville from its cheaper brethren. Virtually nothing obviously interchanged with any other General Motors compact, and the Seville received a level of fit and finish comparable to that of the Fleetwood Brougham. In fact, the Seville was priced significantly higher than any other Cadillac sedan (excepting only the Seventy-Fives) at $12,479. Cadillac officials were anxious that the public not confuse small with cheap, and the Seville was not cheap by any measurement, including fuel economy.[1]

Top, 1975 Calais interior; *bottom*, 1975 Fleetwood Brougham.

This latter issue leads to another important point about this first Seville. It may have been small, but it was far from being an economy car. At this time, the downsized and more fuel-efficient full-size Cadillacs were in final preparation for their 1977 launch. The development of the Seville predated such concerns, however; it was simply a smaller Cadillac conceived in the old manner. It was not particularly space efficient, nor did it deliver fuel economy that was significantly better than the full-size Cadillacs in 1976. It was, however, smartly styled and immediately caught on with the public. A fairly astonishing 60,127 Sevilles were built in the extended 1976 model run. This was, by a good margin, the highest production the Seville would ever achieve.

For the rest of the Cadillac model range, the 1976 model year was one of only modest alterations. There were small, rectangular side marker lights, chrome strips on the cornering lights, and a coarser mesh in the grille. The 1976 Eldorado was mainly distinguished from the previous year by the new, continuous taillight with red lens and large bezel frame. The wheel cover centers were now painted black instead of body color, as in 1975. The Eldorado Biarritz was an-nounced as a mid-year model.

Cadillac production for the year was 304,485, just shy of the 1973 record. Of these 49,184 were Eldorados, including 14,000 convertibles, of which 200 white ones with red-white-and-blue trim—in honor of America's Bicentennial—were absolutely the "last" one.

This occasioned the fantastic "last convertible" hoopla. Cadillac announced that it would cease convertible production with the 1976 Eldorado—it even proclaimed it in the catalog—and the stampede was on. By the time the speculators got through, Eldorado convertibles were selling for as much as double the sticker price. It was a short-lived boom, however, and, by the mid-1980s,

1975 Cadillac supplied to the White House.

with Eldorado convertibles once more in production, a 1976 model was hardly the collectible it was thought to have been at the time.

The reasons Cadillac, and the rest of the manufacturers, decided to cease convertible production, bears some discussion. The first quarter of the 20th Century might aptly be called the "Age of the Open Car." From the dawn of the auto industry at the turn of the century, open cars were so much the rule as to all but exclude closed cars from the marketplace. This came about despite the fact that the roadsters and touring cars then available were rather primitive. They were not really very comfortable, and required elaborate efforts to protect passengers from the vagaries of the weather. These efforts were not only ineffective, but contrary to common sense. If inclement weather is a problem, why not simply close it out of the car and be done with it?

Eventually that is precisely what happened. Hudson introduced the first relatively cheap closed car in 1922 and unleashed a tidal wave of demand for closed cars from the buying public. By the time General Motors launched the first Pontiac in 1926, it was remarkable for having no open models at all in its line.

Then, just when it seemed that open cars were destined to be sacrificed on the altar of "progress" (a term of almost religious impact in pre-Depression America), however, people, and especially those with money, began to recog-

1974 Series Seventy-Five.

nize that the elements were sometimes fun. Closed cars shielded passengers from bad weather it was true, but they were hot and stuffy in the summer and, basically, not much fun. What was needed was a more civilized version of the traditional open car, one that combined the advantages of open and closed driving; in a word, a convertible. What distinguished a true convertible from the old-fashioned touring and roadster types was its roll-down, glass side windows and tight-fitting, folding canvas top.

The early convertibles quickly earned a nickname—"ragtop"—which has stuck with them to this very day, and not without good reason. Modern, flexible, and durable vinyl tops did not become available until the 1950s. Until that time, convertibles were still cold and drafty in the winter (although a quantum improvement over the roadsters and touring cars they replaced), and the canvas had a nasty way of ripping and tearing with age, which, of course, only served to make matters worse. That, together with the inherent squeaks and rattles of the top mechanism, which also became worse with age, made for what our European cousins would refer to as "sporting" transportation.

A turning point in the story came with the development of air conditioning in the 1950s. When that happened, one big reason for convertible ownership disappeared, because air-conditioned cars were just as pleasant to drive during hot weather and had none of the convertible's drawbacks (squeaks, rattles, wind, noise, leaks drafts, etc.).

Convertible production reached all-time peak levels during the mid-1960s. Over half-a-million were produced in 1965, or about 5 percent of total industry production. Air conditioning was gaining dramatically in popularity at the same time, however, and, inevitably, began to eat into ragtop sales in a major way. The decline following that resulted in the end of all major manufacturer convertible production by 1976 (accompanied by all the hoopla surrounding the umpteen thousand "last" Cadillac convertibles that year). Lincoln had dropped out of the field after 1967. American Motors and Imperial had dropped out after 1968. Chrysler built its last convertible in the 1970 model run, Plymouth and Dodge in 1971. Ford and Mercury held on until 1973. Chevrolet, Pontiac, Oldsmobile, and Buick all quit together in 1975.

Detroit evidently thought that the final 1976 Eldorado convertible would be the end of the story. Almost immediately, however, evidence to the contrary started to roll in. The custom conversion houses, who had been principally occupied with manufacturing stretched limousines, began to turn out attractive convertibles using nearly every imaginable chassis. And, although these convertible conversions sold for astronomical premiums over the regular list prices of the cars in-volved, they sold. Furthermore, they sold in numbers that, while limited, were increasing. It seemed inevitable that factory-built—or, at least, factory-authorized—convertibles would appear once more. But, that would take a few more years. In the meantime, Detroit was preoccupied with the ramifications of the fuel shortage gripping the nation and influencing government regulators.

In fact, General Motors, along with the rest of the industry, had been staggered by the fuel crisis. It was something quite unprecedented in American history. Nor could anyone be certain similar shocks would not be coming in the future. America's growing dependence on Middle Eastern sources of petroleum, combined with that region's inherent instability, almost guaranteed a

Top, 1976 Seville interior; *bottom*, 1976 Seville.

long-term threat. So, in 1974, the corporate decision was made to completely redesign the B- and C-body cars for a fall 1976 introduction, with a new "personal" car E-Body to appear for 1979 for the Eldorado (and the related Riviera and Toronado lines). That gave Cadillac two years to re-conceptualize its full-size models, create new designs and engineering, and bring them to market—a tall order, to say the least. Commented Charles M. Jordan, the former Cadillac design chief, then in charge of the General Motors automotive design studios, and, later, General Motors vice-president of design:

> Someday I'm sure we'll look back at the '70s as an era of automotive styling at the crossroads...It's a dramatic turnabout in design.[2]

The 1977 General Motors B/C-body program was not only a dramatic turnabout, it was one of the most successful major programs in the company's entire history. All the car lines resulting from this program came to be regarded as top-notch in terms of design, engineering, and all-important sales appeal. Unlike the similar crash program for the 1959 B-body, there were no duds, no misses, among the 1977 cars. From Chevrolet right up through Cadillac, every division scored a direct hit with its version. The most eloquent proof of this is the simple fact that this basic platform was still in production at Cadillac twenty years later. Historically, there is no other General Motors program that even rivals the 1977 B/C-body for sheer longevity.

For at least twenty years preceding the fuel crisis, American cars had been

1976 Eldorado convertible.

Top, 1977 Fleetwood Brougham; *bottom*, 1977 Seville Eleganté.

getting heavier and bigger. This was a key reason the intermediates sold so well in the 1960s and 1970s; they were similar in size to the traditional "full-size" American family car of the 1940s and 1950s, while the ostensible full-size models attained truly gargantuan proportions. To be sure, there were (and are) many people who measure value by the cubic yard, but the thing that was most curious about American full-size cars circa 1975 was their incredible inefficiency. These cars were big, yes, but they were not particularly roomy. There were some compacts, especially from foreign manufacturers, that could actually rival them for useful interior space: headroom, legroom, and the like —everything but width. The enthusiast magazines had been harping for years that it was not necessary to build a 5,000-pound car to transport four or five adults in comfort. Under pressure, in a program that made wide use of advanced computers, General Motors designers and engineers finally discovered that for themselves.

For Cadillac, the B/C-body program was a deadly serious effort to protect its leadership in the luxury market. Much was at stake as Wayne Kady and his team of designers set about exploring uncharted waters. Kady had been named to head the Cadillac studio just as the 1977 program was launched, and was fully aware that few General Motors divisions had as much to lose as did Cadillac if the ultimate design his team developed failed to meet with public favor. The new bodies were not only trimmer in size, they were far more youthful in appearance than those they replaced. Full rear wheel openings were featured, even on Fleetwoods.[3] The engine was also downsized. A new 425 cubic inch (7.0 liter) V8 became the standard throughout the line,

Introducing the next generation of the luxury car.

Fleetwood Brougham

Coupe deVille

Introducing Cadillac 1977. The brilliant new Fleetwood Brougham with four-wheel disc brakes. The sleek new Coupe deVille. And the stunning new Sedan deVille.

Isn't "next generation" over-stating it? Not at all. This is a totally new Cadillac. Engineered from the ground up for more efficient use of space. New body. New chassis. New suspension system. New frame. New engine.

Building on success. How do you improve a car that consistently has had the highest repeat ownership and the highest resale value of any U.S. luxury car make? Basically, by retaining what you like about Cadillac—the comfort, luxury, security and roominess—and adding to it.

More efficient use of space. There's more rear legroom and

headroom in the DeVilles. Fleetwood Brougham retains the legroom and headroom of its spacious 1976 counterpart. And all have that roomy, Cadillac-size trunk.

Greater fuel economy. In 1977 EPA mileage tests, Cadillac was estimated at 14 miles per gallon city and 18 mpg highway. Your mileage could vary depending upon the type of driving you do, your driving habits, your car's condition and available equipment.

It's a lively generation. Here, in Cadillac 1977, is an agile luxury car. Quick to respond. With pickup—all-around performance—that could surprise you. There's more maneuverability for easier parking and a more confident feel in city traffic.

Even more comfort and convenience. There's a new instru-

ment panel that organizes things for you. New easy-entry/easy-exit door design. Match mounting of tires and wheels for a superb ride. And a seat belt you can conveniently draw across your lap any way you like.

To protect your investment. The 1977 Cadillacs are designed to battle rattles and rust. Extensive rust-fighting measures include anti-corrosion inner front fender panels. And widespread use of Zincrometal® and bimetal (stainless steel on aluminum).

A ride you won't believe . . . until you take a test drive. As your Cadillac dealer, we would be happy to arrange it.

And for a different kind of luxury . . . you might consider the international-size Seville by Cadillac . . . or the 1977 Eldorado with front-wheel drive.

1977 Cadillac newspaper advertisement.

even on the old-size Eldorado (the Seville remained a special case and continued to use its 350 V8). The Eldorado and Seville received new grilles and headlights. The Calais series was dropped, although there is some evidence that this was a last-minute decision, and the limousine terminology was changed —seven-passenger sedans became "limousines" and limousines became "formal limousines."

In terms of efficiency, there was no comparison with past practices. While shedding hundreds of pounds, around a foot of length, and 8.5 inches of wheelbase (11.5 inches on the Brougham), the 1977 Cadillacs had more headroom front and rear, more rear seat legroom, and more luggage space. True, the new bodies were somewhat narrower and this impacted somewhat on shoulder room, but increases in most other dimensions, combined with greatly increased maneuverability, more than compensated. Fuel economy, of course, was the reason for the program in the first place, and constituted yet another benefit.

A longer term effect, and benefit, of the 1977 B-body program was to redirect thinking within General Motors. Efficiency and ergonomics suddenly rose to the top of the list of priorities. To be sure, there have been misfires in model programs since 1977, and these values have sometimes been poorly understood or applied, but, as a direct result of the changes in thinking that started with the 1977 B/C program, General Motors cars of all types today are dramatically more efficient at whatever they are intended to do than ever before. It was a true watershed for General Motors and for Cadillac.

Most satisfying of all, Cadillac production reached a new record in 1977: 358,487 cars were built, including 264,785 of the new down-sized models. It was not an unalloyed triumph, though, for Lincoln sales rose sharply on the strength of a new Mark V and on disaffection among luxury car buyers, who either weren't ready to think efficiently or were determined to grab at one (perhaps) last chance to buy a traditional luxury car. A rather spectacular total of 191,335 Lincolns were built during the 1977 model run, including 80,321 examples of the new Mark V. Sugar plums were suddenly dancing before the eyes of Ford Motor Company officials, who thought they just might be coming within range of the arch enemy at last.

There was a major marketing disaster recorded for the marque, as well. The Lincoln response to the Seville challenge had been urgently prepared, if only to prove to the public that Lincoln could build smaller cars just as well as Cadillac, if it really wanted to do so. The downsizing of the big Lincoln and the Mark was a different matter. After much heated debate, it was decided that the big Lincolns would not be shrunk until 1980.

Top, 1978 Sedan de Ville with Phaeton option; *bottom*, 1978 Eldorado Custom Biarritz.

The compact Lincoln Versailles was announced to the public on March 28, 1977. The reception was a distinctly cool one. Lincoln officials had reasoned that since the Seville was based on the General Motors NOVA shell, it would be perfectly acceptable to base the Versailles on the Ford Granada/Mercury Monarch shell. They failed to take into account, however, the extent to which Cadillac had differentiated the Seville from its cheaper brethren, whereas the Versailles looked for all the world like a Granada with a Mark grille and a tire hump rather awkwardly grafted on the back. The buyers stayed away in droves despite the fact that the Versailles was priced a couple of thousand dollars below the Seville.

The 1978 model year was a sort of calm between the storms at Cadillac. The major product launches of 1976 and 1977 needed to be consolidated before the next major pushes in 1979 and 1980. So, there were few changes to the 1978 Cadillacs. New grilles were in evidence all around, and a few pieces of trim modified here and there.

There were, however, a spate of new models in all product lines. The Se-

1979 Eldorado Biarritz.

ville got a jazzed-up Eleganté (which sold for the then astronomical price of $17,310), the Eldorado got the Custom Biarritz Classic, and the DeVilles got the phaeton roof. This latter option involved a pseudo-convertible roof by means of convertible-type fabric in place of the vinyl roof. It was designed to answer the growing demands of Cadillac customers for a return of the rag-tops, or, at least, a return to ragtop styling. A significant engineering development that Cadillac would certainly like to forget appeared on the scene at mid-year, as well. The 350 cubic inch (5.7 liter) General Motors diesel engine was introduced in the Seville series.

Total Cadillac production exploded to a new record in 1978: 350,813 cars were built. Best of all, Lincoln sales were down as the culture shock of down-sizing wore off and the public began to accept the new General Motors products in a big way.

The big news at Cadillac in 1979 was the downsizing of the Eldorado; the Seville would follow in 1980 using the same platform (although designated as the K-body) and drive-train. The Eldorados were built on the new General Motors E-Body and featured four-wheel independent suspension, a remarkable thing on an American car in 1979. Power was supplied by a new 350 cubic inch (5.7 liter) engine (not the diesel, although it came from the same engine family and was joined by the diesel version as an extra-cost option). They were beautifully appointed inside and featured exterior styling that won instant raves from most luxury car buyers. Two regular models were listed: the Eldorado and the Eldorado Biarritz. The cabriolet roof was still listed as an option. Total Eldorado production soared to an all-time record which still stands: 67,437 cars for the model year. In fact, the grand total of 381,113 Cadillacs of all types built during the 1979 model run was also an all-time record that (as of this writing) still stands.

As with the downsized full-size cars, Cadillac scored a direct hit with its version of the new E-Body, the last such triumph the division would experience for many years. The 1979 series Eldorado, which remained in production essentially unchanged until 1985 (except for powerplants, which rotated almost annually for the first several years), grabbed leadership of the luxury personal car field back from the Mark Lincolns and are deserving of considerable credit for that. They were beautifully finished, sensibly sized vehicles for their times.

But, times were about to turn sticky again. The Iranian fuel crisis choked-off sales in the spring, and helped throw the nation into a severe recession that would last until 1982 and test the mettle of all automobile manufacturers, but especially those in the luxury field. Cadillac had been through some tough times in its history and survived, but the most serious testing period of all was about to unfold.

1979 "Gucci" Seville.

CHAPTER EIGHT

1980 Seville.

Crisis in Paradise:
1980–84

AS THE CURTAIN ROSE on a new decade at the start of the 1980 model year, one of the great dramas in automotive history began at Cadillac. Despite the upbeat pronouncements emanating with clock-like regularity from Clark Street, despite the slick confidence displayed year-after-year in Cadillac advertising, despite the sense of prosperous normality on view at friendly neighborhood Cadillac dealers from coast-to-coast, the division was in deep trouble by the mid-1980s. Even today, it is fighting with everything it has to recover from the manifold blunders and missed opportunities of that period, and regain the luxury market supremacy it enjoyed virtually uncontested for decades. A combination of bad luck and bad habits had ill-equipped the division for the challenges it suddenly faced.

As late as 1960, Cadillac accounted for better than 80 percent of all luxury cars sold in the Unites States. This dominance lasted through the 1970s, although increasing competition from Lincoln—and to a lesser, but growing, extent the European luxury brands—whittled down the margin. Then, from 1980 to 1990, Lincoln shaved Cadillac's once untouchable lead in sales from a margin of three-to-one to near parity. In June of 1990, Lincoln nearly out-sold Cadillac nationally for the first time in history. Although this proved to be an anomaly, it gave an unmistakable indication of how close the contest had become. Those charged with Lincoln's fortunes were quick to claim credit for this, and it was true that Lincoln led Ford Motor Company's quest for higher standards that made that company the recognized leader in quality in Detroit. Dramatically improved quality notwithstanding, though, Lincoln design and marketing efforts were decidedly uneven in this period. The all-new 1980 Town Car was a near disaster when first announced, the 1982 Compact Continental was a major disappointment, and the 1984 Mark VII received raves from the automotive press, but a tepid reception from Lincoln buyers. Of Lincoln's four major new product launches during the decade, only the 1988 Continental won a measure of popular support at its introduction.

So, what happened to cause this turn of events at Cadillac? It is not to belittle Lincoln's efforts during the 1980s, or those of Cadillac's foreign competitors, to say that Cadillac's decline was due almost entirely to problems at Cadillac.

To be sure, some of these critical problems were external—i.e., they originiated outside the division. The fuel crises of the 1970s had repeatedly altered market conditions, forcing all automakers to scramble as best they could to develop smaller and more fuel-efficient models in wildly fluctuating market conditions. The compact Cimarron, introduced by Cadillac in 1982, was a particularly clumsy attempt to do that. The downsized 1985 DeVille/Fleetwood series, conceived with this same mind-set, was better, but arrived just as the market for traditional-size luxury cars was rebounding. Lincoln, which simply did not have the money to develop new models during this period, was forced to stick with the 1980-series Town Car. That "strategy"—such as it was—proved to be a gold mine when the big car boom returned in the middle of the decade.

Still, all-too-many of Cadillac's problems were entirely homegrown. The rear-drive Brougham was so completely de-emphasized when the smaller, front-drive DeVilles and Fleetwoods were first announced, that many long-time Cadillac buyers switched over to Lincoln in the mistaken belief that Cadillac no longer offered a traditional-size luxury sedan. The stretched derivative of the Brougham, however—the traditional Cadillac factory-built limousine—was, indeed, dropped. Again, Lincoln rushed in to capitalize on Cadillac's abdication, and a market that for decades had been virtually a Cadillac monopoly saw a shift in the dominant player.

Next, Cadillac's high profit Eldorado and Seville lines were given disastrous new body styling in 1986 that sent paying customers away in droves. Initial slow sales of these models (and the related Olds Toronado and Buick Riviera) reportedly cost General Motors half-a-billion-dollars-a-year in bottom line profits in the latter part of the decade. Meanwhile, at the other end of the scale, the mid-priced Cimarron—in many ways a metaphor for the division in this era—was seriously diluting Cadillac's hard-won prestige.

Still another nagging problem was the disturbing drop in Cadillac quality. The modular engine introduced in 1981 as an effort to improve fuel economy —the notorious V8-6-4—was quickly scrapped, but not before it severely tarnished Cadillac's once sterling reputation for engineering excellence. General Motors' wretched diesel produced further luxury car buyer alienation, even though Cadillac had little or nothing to do with its engineering. In addition, the Lake Orion, Michigan, plant (completed in 1984 to build the front-drive DeVilles, and Fleetwoods), and the Hamtramck plant (completed a year later for the Eldorado, Seville, and Allanté), simply did not function at acceptable quality standards when first brought on line. Once again, Cadillac paid the enormous price in customer dissatisfaction.

As if more trouble were needed, a further body blow was landed in 1984 when General Motors' chairman, Roger Smith, imposed a sweeping corporate reorganization that centralized all engineering, design, and manufacturing operations within the corporation. The functional result was to reduce the automotive divisions to little more than marketing entities, depriving divisional managers of control over most of the essential elements in creating the cars they were expected to sell.

Things began to fall apart for Cadillac in 1980. In this, Cadillac was not entirely alone. Chrysler was on the verge of bankruptcy and the whole industry was reeling from the full effects of the second gasoline crisis prompted by the Iranian revolution, which had come too late to do more than skim a little of the icing off the cake in the 1979 model run. Not so for 1980. The crisis, whose effects were compounded by Carter Administration fuel allocation bungling, first frightened buyers away from full-size luxury cars and high performance cars, in general, then set the severe 1980–82 recession in motion, which frightened everyone else.

For both Cadillac and Lincoln, the 1980 models were announced just in time for the onset of the recession, and a crushing rise in interest rates that saw the prime rate break 20 percent—two-and-a-half times the traditional level. As the gloom from the gas crisis together with high interest rates discouraged traditional luxury car buyers, sales of full-size cars collapsed by the middle of the 1980 model year. The division was thrown into turmoil, and began frantically searching for ways to stop what it feared was a permanent downward spiral. Spurred on by widely-believed predictions of recurring fuel shortages and $3-per-gallon gasoline, Cadillac planners instituted a crash program to develop products they hoped would ensure the survival of the division in the 1980s, and beyond. The pervasive sense of doom on Clark Street at this time cannot be overstated, for it alone explains the actions taken over the next several years—actions that would, ultimately, come back to haunt the division.

The drop in sales during the 1980 model year certainly wasn't for want of effort. Except for the Eldorado, which was a carry-over line, the Cadillac story was one of significant changes across the board. The engine was downsized yet again, to 6.0 liters (368 cubic inches), and the DeVilles and Fleetwoods were cleverly restyled in response to what was thought to be the temper of the times. When the 1977 down-sized General Motors full-size cars were introduced, many customers had complained that they looked too small. Heeding that concern, Cadillac's designers set to work making the reskinned 1980 models look bigger. It was mostly done with mirrors—the 1980 full-size cars were actually lighter and more fuel efficient than before—but the illusion worked all too well.

The K-body Seville—which, except for unique interior and rear-end styling, was essentially a four-door Eldorado—was memorable for being of the short-lived "razorback" school of design. Developed by Hooper & Company in England in the 1930s, the pronounced downward curve of the beltline met a dramatic concave downward sweep at the rear window, and combined to give a racy look (and a characteristic trunk bulge) to the rather boxy Rolls-Royce of the day. Cadillac revived the style when it wanted a "classic" look for this, its second-generation Seville. Chrysler also picked it up for the last-gasp Imperial coupe built in very small numbers between 1981 and 1983, and Lincoln was destined to jump on the bandwagon with its compact Continental in the 1982 model year.

Designers at all three companies experienced problems in translating the razorback onto the lower and wider proportions of contemporary cars. Cadillac effected the purest evocation of the style in 1980, then, flinching in the face of tepid public response, tried to de-emphasize the trunk bulge with a wide beltline molding from 1981 on. The Continental went Cadillac one better with body sculpturing that emphasized the beltline even more. The result on both cars was an odd-looking convex beltline curve that made them look hunched in the middle, rather like a cat with its back up. Chrysler designers didn't bother with the beltline curve at all, but still ended up with a surprisingly pleasing result that nonetheless failed to attract noticeable numbers of paying customers.[1]

The Seville's daring was not limited to its styling, either. It had the dubious distinction of being the only Cadillac model ever in which a diesel engine was listed as standard equipment—specifically, the notorious GM 350 cubic inch diesel—although the Cadillac 6.0 liter gasoline engine was a no-cost option.

The General Motors diesel program was another product of the contemporary obsession with fuel efficiency and, without question, was one of the worst disasters in the corporation's history. Sadly, Cadillac did a big business in diesels in the 1979–82 period when most of the 144,000 diesel-equipped Cadillacs were built. In fairness to Cadillac, the division did not design the diesel which originated (more-or-less) at Oldsmobile, and the public was screaming for them in 1979 and 1980. General Motors began to develop enormous plant capacity for future diesel production, while Cadillac officials expansively projected that 80 percent or more of their production would be diesels by 1985. When, however, the basic design flaws in the Olds diesel became known, demand collapsed overnight. Cadillac built just over 42,000 diesel cars in the 1981 model year, and barely 5,000 in 1983. After 1985, the option was deleted, but not before the division unwittingly cultivated tens of thousands of disgruntled owners, many of whom never bought another Cadillac.[2]

Fortunately for Cadillac, Lincoln was having its own problems. The design of the 1980 series Lincolns and Marks was carefully crafted, and there is every indication that the final result was just what Ford and Lincoln-Mercury officials had wanted—which recalls the old saying about being careful what you wish for, because you may get it. While it definitely looked like a Lincoln, it was a fairly awkward example of the late Seventies "square" school of design prevalent at Ford. This style had first been seen in the successful 1977 Fairmont/Zephyr series compacts, but later reached the point of self-caricature in the disastrous Thunderbird/Cougar models introduced for 1979. The 1980 series Lincoln Continentals and Marks were not quite so bad, but they were far from well received in the marketplace.

The Mark series was expanded to include a four-door sedan for the first time. Both, however, were thinly disguised Town Cars/Coupes and shared virtually everything save minor trim details with their cheaper, less prestigious brethren. The 1980 Versailles was not changed in any major way. This was slated to be its final year, in any case, and Ford probably could not wait to see it go.

The Cadillac DeVilles and Fleetwoods suffered, too, so Lincoln was by no means alone in its misery, but the collapse of full-size Lincoln sales was significantly worse than that suffered by Cadillac and provided much of what little lift there was for the DeVille. So poor was the public's early response to the redesigned Town Car that, for the next several years, it survived largely on massive fleet sales to rental car companies. The absence of a competitive compact luxury car was clearly hurting Lincoln, too, as the Seville and Eldorado were the only relative bright spots for Cadillac.

A total of 231,028 Cadillacs were built during the 1980 model run, down nearly 40 percent from the level of the previous year. Eldorado production declined to 52,685, but it emerged as the clear leader in the personal luxury car market. Seville production sagged to 39,344, which was still a less precipitous drop than that experienced by the Eldorado, but, nearly 37 percent of the Sevilles built were diesel equipped.

The next year, 1981, saw few design changes in any of the Cadillac models, the most significant being the addition of a Fleetwood coupe (which had actually been a mid-year announcement in the 1980 model run). Nevertheless, Cadillac production rose a bit, to 240,189 cars for the model year.

The big news for the 1981 model year was the "modular displacement" V8-6-4 engine designed to shut down unneeded cylinders at cruising speeds. In introducing this engine to the press corps, General Manager Kennard described it as a "major" engineering achievement that would provide Cadillac customers with "one of the most advanced, dependable, and efficient production automobiles in the world." The 1981 Cadillac sales brochure assured prospects that the V8-6-4 "has been proven in over a half-million miles of testing; it's that reliable." Would that it had been true.

The basic concept behind the V8-6-4 was that the enormous power of a modern V8 was used mostly during acceleration. At cruising speeds a mere

1981 Eldorado Biarritz.

Top, 1981 Eldorado Brougham coupe; *bottom*, 1981 Fleetwood Brougham.

fraction of the available power was needed. So, Cadillac engineers devised a computer microprocessor that would shut down fuel flow to unneeded cylinders as throttle load decreased, from eight cylinders, to six, to four at highway speeds. Any sudden burst of acceleration would instantly reactivate the feathered cylinders. That, at any rate, was the theory. Unfortunately the system, quickly earned a bad reputation due to an epidemic of computer malfunctions. Cadillac's reputation suffered seriously, as did the resale value of V8-6-4-equipped cars.[3]

The real irony of the V8-6-4 fiasco was that, even when it was working properly, it offered relatively little benefit. The combined city/highway EPA fuel economy rating of the standard 368 V8 was 15 miles-per-gallon; the V8-6-4 raised this to around 17. The 4.1 liter (252 cubic inch) Buick V6 that was offered as an option in DeVilles and Fleetwoods (excepting the limousines) late in the year in 1980, then expanded to the Seville and Eldorado lines for 1981, made even less sense. It was officially rated at 18 miles-per-gallon, but was so over-stressed in Cadillac application that it actually delivered worse fuel economy than the V8-6-4. It was a sign of the level of desperation at the division that it was willing to try anything that even appeared to improve fuel economy, regardless of the practical result.

Cadillac's focus on repositioning itself reached its low ebb with the launch of the compact J-car Cimarron in the summer of 1981 as a 1982 model. Based all-too-obviously on the low-buck Chevrolet Cavalier, the Cimarron commit-

Top, 1982 Cimarron interior; *bottom*, 1982 Cimarron.

1982 Cimarron newspaper ad.

ted every mistake Lincoln had made with the ill-fated and unlamented Versailles—only worse. In fact, next to the Cimarron, the Versailles looked like a work of masterful execution.

Cadillac management had begged its way into the J-car program barely a year before the Cimarron was announced to the public. This meant, as a practical matter, that the division was forced to accept the car "as is" with only the most minor alterations to attempt to make it look like a Cadillac. General Motors' president, Pete Estes, warned Kennard, "Ed, you don't have time to

1982 Cadillac hearse by A.H.A. in Toronto.

turn the J-car into a Cadillac." Estes was right. Simply put, the Cimarron was a Chevrolet Cavalier with a Cadillac grille insert and Cadillac badges. Even car "nuts" had to get close enough to read the badges to tell the two cars apart. True, the Cimarron featured some minor suspension tweaks, leather upholstery, and every available J-car option as standard equipment, but the $12,000 asking price did not buy much in the way of Cadillac distinction. One point lost in most discussions about the J-car, though, is that it was not merely a second-rate Cadillac, it was a second-rate car, at least in its 1982 form. With the original 1.8 liter engine, it was grossly under-powered. Worse, the automatic transmission was so poorly matched that it simply magnified the engine's shortcomings, while the four-speed manual—which, on paper, should have been a viable alternative—felt as if it had been supplied by John Deere.

Technically, it should be pointed out, the 1982 Cimarron was not a Cadillac. It was marketed as the "Cimarron by Cadillac" and salesmen were trained to correct customers who innocently referred to it as a Cadillac. This indicated a certain nervousness on the part of the division (well-founded, as it turned out). Beginning in the 1983 model year, the silly pretense was discarded, but Cadillac dealers were still stuck selling an over-priced Cavalier whose main "Cadillac" distinction was limited to its leather interior.[4]

The division had hoped that the Cimarron would appeal to "near luxury" buyers in the BMW 3-series class, but the last thing they wanted was a clunky General Motors J-car. Cadillac's traditional clientele felt much the same way. As a result, the division's confident predictions of 20,000 Cimarrons during the remainder of the 1981 model year and 50,000 per year thereafter came a cropper. Only 8,786 were built during 1981 and a paltry 14,889 found buyers in 1982.

The Cimarron program was a disaster on many levels. Taken at face value, it failed to attract the "foreign intenders" for whom it was ostensibly targeted. Overall, sales failed to reach even one-third of the division's forecasts. It triggered the major slide in Cadillac's prestige that was to gain disturbing momentum over the next four years. And, it was the final evidence that Cadillac management had simply lost its sense of direction. Since 1980, in its frenzy to do something—anything—to get the division moving, management had tried

Top, 1982 Eldorado Touring Coupe; *bottom*, 1982 HT 4100 engine.

selling half-baked modular displacement technology, Olds-built diesels, Buick-built V6s, and, finally, fresh-out-of-the-box Chevrolets.

Having done all the damage it could in 1981, the division had better news to report when the 1982 Cadillacs were announced. There was an interesting new model. The Eldorado Touring Coupe featured "black-out" bright work, a beefed-up suspension, bucket seats, and a console. Silver was the only color available at first, but black was a mid-year option. The Touring Coupe was yet another effort to reach import buyers with a better-handling Cadillac. Eldorado base prices in 1982 started at $18,716, while the Touring Coupe listed for $20,666.

Although the rest of the Cadillac product line was little changed, once again there was a new engine. The late, unlamented 368 cubic inch V8-6-4 was replaced by a smaller, fuel-injected, 4.1 liter V8 (except, again, in the limousines), labeled the HT 4100.[5] A new four-speed automatic overdrive transmission was also featured.

Unlike the V8-6-4, the HT 4100 engine was basically sound in its engineering. Also unlike the V8-6-4, the HT 4100 was too little engine for the car and suffered from the same power-to-weight problems of the 4.1 liter Buick V6 (which remained on the option list).[6] The HT 4100 was designed for the coming downsized DeVilles and Fleetwoods, which were scheduled as 1983 models. They were destined to be delayed repeatedly, and the appearance of the HT 4100 suggests the original target date may have been 1982. In any event, the HT 4100 was a decidedly sluggish performer in the old models. It also suffered from a distressing number of teething troubles at first (oil leakage, primarily), while the four-speed automatic overdrive transmission earned an early reputation for unreliability, too, before it also got sorted out. On top of the diesels and the V8-6-4, this was not the kind of word-of-mouth Cadillac needed. Perhaps not entirely by coincidence, this was the year that Lincoln Town Car sales at last began to show upward movement. Overall, Cadillac production declined slightly to 235,584, partly under the weight of the worst economic recession in forty years.

Apparently, Cadillac management was not alone in thinking that full-size cars were doomed. Lincoln took its most honored name and placed it on the compact replacement for the unlamented Versailles. The 1982 Continental was a first class effort throughout and showed that Ford had learned its marketing lessons from the Versailles program. Projected production for the Continental—40,000 for the 1982 run—was missed by a wide margin, but it was still about 20 percent better than the Seville's performance that year. In truth, none of the three cars offering razorback design were notably successful—

Seville, Imperial, or Continental. Not even the addition of a powder-blue "Frank Sinatra Edition" to the Imperial line, complete with no less than 16 cassette tapes recorded by "Old Blue Eyes" himself, could produce an upturned sales curve there, but the Continental came off best overall, at least commercially. Production figures for 1982 show 23,908 Continentals, which compared favorably to the 19,998 Sevilles and the almost invisible 2,540 Imperials produced, making Lincoln the sales leader in this small market segment. Overall, Lincoln production was up 22 percent. Lincoln was back from the dead—barely.

There was a significant management change at Cadillac's helm in 1982. In September, Ed Kennard stepped down after eight years. His replacement was Robert D. Burger, who had been vice-president of the General Motors marketing staff since 1977.

The DeVilles and Fleetwoods were nearly unchanged for 1983, with trim alterations being about the extent of it. This is not surprising as these lines were supposed to have been replaced that year. The Eldorado Touring Coupe was now available in Sonora Saddle Firemist in addition to Sable Black. The much-vaunted General Motors Delco-Bose sound system was now an option. Cabriolet roof treatments—similar to the 1970s phaeton roofs—were announced for the Eldorado and Seville at mid-year. The Cimarron D'Oro was another special model announced at mid-year. Essentially, a monochromatic black color option featuring gold (replacing chrome) trim, the D'Oro was not widely publicized.

Total Cadillac production nonetheless rose as the nation's economy at last emerged from the bruising recession. A total of 292,814 were built. If the Seville was doing poorly against the Continental, the Eldorado had gained unquestioned supremacy in the personal luxury coupe segment, outselling the Mark Lincolns by about two-to-one. This fact was not lost on Ford Motor Company, and a dramatically different Mark VII was in the wings being prepared for 1984.

One intriguing non-factory model in 1983 had been Hess and Eisenhardt's semi-custom Eldorado convertible. Hess and Eisenhardt was an old-line professional car builder (hearses and ambulances, primarily, although limousines were built, too) based in Cincinnati, Ohio. Their convertible conversion was thoughtfully executed and suited the Eldorado's design marvelously well. Cadillac must have thought so, too, for it offered the conversion as a factory model beginning in the 1984 model year.

So, after all the fanfare surrounding its "last" convertible in 1976, Cadillac was back at it as if it had completely forgotten its promise of "never again."

For those who still doubted the fundamental tenets of Christian theology, Cadillac's proof that there was life after death must have been of considerable comfort. A few owners of 1976 Eldorado convertibles had a different view, though, and there were numerous threats of litigation that ultimately came to nothing.[7]

The rest of the 1984 Cadillac line was virtually a verbatim repeat of 1983,

Top, 1983 Fleetwood Brougham interior; *bottom*, 1983 Coupe de Ville.

with only the most insignificant trim alterations to distinguish the new models from the old. Model year production, however, rose modestly to just over 300,000 cars, but the picture was confused somewhat by the mid-year introduction (finally) of the down-sized DeVilles and Fleetwoods, which were officially considered to be 1985s.

There was one truly special 1984 Cadillac that deserves mention. Begin-

Top, 1983 Eldorado Biarritz interior; *bottom*, 1983 Seville Eleganté interior.

ning in the 1980s, most likely due to the enormous costs involved in producing Presidential parade cars to contemporary specifications, Ford Motor Company and General Motors unofficially divided up the responsibility. Lincolns had been in general White House use since the 1930s, but, in 1984, Cadillac supplied the parade car used during most of the Reagan era.

There was significant competitive news, too. Lincoln announced its new Mark VII. The styling was controversial. The first Lincoln product to follow the new Ford aero school of design, the Mark VII was entirely too similar to the related Ford Thunderbird and Mercury Cougar models, with which it even shared a few exterior sheet metal panels until the 1987 T-Bird/Cougar restyling. The LSC version, on the other hand, which went after the enthusiast market hammer and tong, deleted the plastic wood and substituted excellent leather-covered, multiple-adjustment seats, and the high output edition of Ford's 5.0 liter V8. Numerous chassis refinements completed the LSC package and prompted raves from the motoring press. Despite its virtues (or possibly because of them), the 33,344 cars actually built in 1984 failed to come close to the original projection of 45,000, making the Mark VII the third consecutive Lincoln product launch that had been a serious disappointment.

1984 Fleetwood Brougham d'Elegance.

1984 Eldorado with cabriolet roof.

Worse, Mark VII production fell far below the 77,806 Cadillac Eldorados built that year—and the Eldorado was in its sixth year on its current body.

The Mark VII's main failing may have been that it stretched the envelope too far for its existing customer base, but it had also earned new respect for Lincoln from enthusiasts, import fanciers, and younger people who would be driving the luxury market in the 1990s, and beyond. In the final analysis, the Mark VII was a modest commercial failure, but an honorable one that probably advanced Lincoln's prospects in a significant way over the long run and pointed toward a new direction that Cadillac would ignore at its peril.

That potential threat would be the worry of Cadillac's new general manager. Bob Burger moved on to Chevrolet in January, 1984, to be replaced by John O. Grettenberger. Grettenberger, a tall, silver-haired, authoritatively handsome man, had started as a clerk in Oldsmobile's Los Angeles zone office in 1963. He had worked his way up through the corporate system in positions that covered the full range of sales and marketing tasks. Along the way, he served as a special marketing consultant for Isuzu Motors in Japan and as director of sales of General Motors' Opel division in Germany. By 1983, he had risen to be director of all of Oldsmobile's product, strategic, and business planning. He was prepared for a challenging opportunity in top management and, at Cadillac, he was to get it—and, no doubt, a lot more than he bargained for besides. His first challenge came from "downtown," from GM's headquarters on Detroit's West Grand Boulevard.

Probably no event in the American auto industry in the past quarter-century has been as controversial as the 1984 reorganization of General Motors. Many industry observers still regard it with disapproval bordering on contempt. The conventional wisdom is that General Motors took something that was not broken, decided to fix it anyway—then botched the job. On the other hand, others feel that it did not go far enough. In general, though, it has come to be regarded as a botched job and General Motors' then-chairman, Roger Smith, has been widely discredited as its prime author. The truth, as is usually the case, is quite a bit more complicated.

1984 Presidential limousine.

1984 Presidential limousine interior.

William C. Durant, General Motors' founder, had failed in part because he was unwilling or unable to bring some order to the operating divisions. Thus, by 1920, General Motors was a chaotic group of autonomous car companies acting, for the most part, in direct competition with each other while ignoring important market segments the corporation had to reach in order to survive. The original management structure that Alfred Sloan had instituted in the 1920s to remedy the situation was military in its outlines. The operating divisions were like armies and were given wide latitude to act within their individual spheres of influence, while corporate management would determine those spheres, set broad strategy, and mediate between the divisions where necessary. The scheme worked brilliantly in the 1920s, but began to suffer under the crushing weight of the Depression when Buick and Oldsmobile were permitted to move down into Pontiac's market segment in search of customers. Systemic inefficiencies and distortions since World War II had slowly overtaken the corporation, as well, and, by 1980, the entire organization was in confusion. As we have seen, Cadillac was floundering in this era, but so were the other automotive divisions, and so was the corporation as a whole.

In theory, Grettenberger was completely responsible for the design, engineering, and manufacture of all Cadillac products. This had been arguably the case when Nick Dreystadt was in charge from 1934 to 1946, although, even then, Cadillac bought its bodies from Fisher, and had to share bodies and components with other car divisions (particularly Buick). Within limits, however, Dreystadt exercised considerable control over his "company" and was largely responsible for its success or failure; i.e., profitability.

After World War II, the spread of General Motors assembly plants across the nation, under the control of the General Motors Assembly Division (known by the wonderfully evocative acronym, GMAD, which was pronounced "gee-mad"), steadily diluted divisional control of the manufacturing end of the business. The elimination of tariff barriers with Canada in the 1960s added General Motors' Canadian plants to the brew. By the time Grettenberger arrived on the scene, every single Cadillac product line was slated to be built someplace else in the sprawling General Motors empire by the summer of 1985. Worse, most Cadillacs were, to some extent, badge-engineered cars in which the division's design and engineering input had been in varying degrees limited. (Often, as with the Cimarron, extremely limited.)[8] In addition, transfer pricing—the cost-plus basis upon which General Motors divisions historically conducted business with each other—had so distorted the financial picture as to make any true accountability impossible. William E. Hoglund, who rose through the ranks at Pontiac to become general manager in 1980 and was destined to exert crucial influence over Cadillac, recalled:

1984 Seville with cabriolet roof.

Transfer pricing screwed up any evaluation of the division on a profit basis. Even within GMAD, we [Pontiac] paid Chevrolet more for the Ventura than they charged their dealers for the Nova. We paid Chevrolet more, when they were out of Lordstown, for the Firebird than they charged their dealers for the Camaro. They charged us more for the Sunbird than they charged their dealers for the Monza.[9]

Chevrolet could get away with that because the official pricing policy—established back in the 1920s—dictated that one General Motors division selling to another would charge "only" for the cost of the component or service—plus ten percent. The rub was that the division doing the selling determined the cost, so all divisions became adept at loading costs onto components they sold to each other. Again, Hoglund explained:

> They allocate the whole cost to Pontiac and then they put ten percent on
> that! So, we had variable losses on Firebirds, Sunbirds, and the X-car, which
> we called the Phoenix. Every one we sold, we lost more money. My guess
> is that in 1978, when we sold a record number of vehicles, we lost money
> because the high volume cars were cars we lost money on. We sold 200,000
> Firebirds and lost money on every one of them.[10]

The same thing was happening to Cadillac. This had been a limited issue in Dreystadt's day, but the growing inter-dependence of General Motors' operating divisions in the postwar era had dramatically changed the landscape. Still, one wonders, how could an operating division survive selling products upon which it lost money? Hoglund:

> We were, at that point, justifying product programs based on corporate profit-
> ability. There wasn't any divisional profitability involved. Delco-Remy's making
> money on the battery. Packard Electric on the wiring harness. Guide Lamp
> on the taillamps. And, on and on. So, you take that component profitability,
> which in those days was very rich, again because of transfer pricing, and add
> to it Fisher Body's huge margins, and so on a cost standpoint all the cars were
> doing fine, but on [the] books they were a disaster. But, nobody took the books
> seriously. You couldn't. It was all funny-money. It was a joke.[11]

The role of a general manager had changed so much over the years as to become virtually unrecognizable. At its worst, the distortions in the system had put more emphasis on selling components to other GM divisions than to pleasing the ultimate consumer. Hoglund continued:

> You were not running a total business because of this inter-dependence. We
> were buying and selling so much stuff among each other that the divisions
> were making more money on the stuff they sold to GM's divisions than they

were on stuff they were selling to dealers. It was a never-never land. We had to do the reorganization because we had gone so far that we had lost the concept of accountability and responsibility.[12]

Even so, the decision to reorganize was not an easy one. It developed following a period of tentative mini-reorganizations and considerable soul-searching within General Motors. Robert C. Stempel, then general manager of Chevrolet and eventually chairman of General Motors, recalled:

> The announcement that came in '84 was after an awful lot of rationalization at the top of the corporation. And, then, that last year a number of us were invited in to say, "Hey, do you guys buy into this? Because you're going to be here long after we are, and once you undo Fisher Body you can't put it back together. Once you undo the car divisions you can't bring it back." The top leaders at General Motors were really agonizing: "Do we want to leave all these years of history behind us and do it this new way?" My own personal opinion is thank goodness we did.[13]

It is an opinion by no means universally shared. The reorganization greatly streamlined General Motors operations, although even in restructured form General Motors remained a huge and enormously complex company. Briefly described, the North American car divisions (excepting Saturn) were reorganized into two groups: Chevrolet-Pontiac-General Motors Canada (CPC) and Buick-Oldsmobile-Cadillac (B-O-C). Truck and other commercial operations were combined into the Truck & Bus Group. GMAD and Fisher Body were disbanded, and their operations were divided among the groups. The groups were responsible for engineering and manufacturing the various vehicle lines, while divisions, such as Cadillac, were reduced to being little more than marketing departments with authority over sales, service, parts, and other after-the-sale operations. Stempel, who was named to head the Buick-Oldsmobile-Cadillac Group following the reorganization, defended the system thusly in a 1991 interview:

> The general manager today has the marketing function and [the decision as to] what he wants his car to be. Yes, he has to work very closely with the car building group and the car building group may be building cars for three general managers, [but] it's their responsibility to make sure that they meet each of the general manager's specs. The general manager can focus on marketing, on customer satisfaction, on things that are important to the brand character of his division. I can't emphasize that enough, because he's dealing with other competitors in the marketplace that are market-driven. The car building groups want to take their product and be sure that they meet the general manager's expectation. They're marketing to the general

manager, his demographics, and so on. And they're going to tailor that car. So, we depend on the general manager to make sure his cars are tailored to potential owners. That's really his job, and it's a full-time job. The second big piece of it, of course, is his dealer body. He's able to spend more time with his dealers. And for all of us, that's really a key piece of the action today.[14]

In short, the General Motors system had become increasingly non-functional and the 1984 reorganization was intended to restore efficient lines of authority and, with it, meaningful concepts of responsibility and accountability. But, as soon as it was announced, there were those—including many within the corporation—who felt that the effort had gone too far, that in "streamlining" the corporation in such a way as to limit the control of a general manager over his products, inevitable pressure was created that, in time, would make it difficult to maintain individual brand identity.

In the meantime, the first 1985 Cadillac products (or the last 1983 products, considering their repeated delays) made it to dealer showrooms. The new down-sized C-body cars—known to Cadillac, Buick, and Olds dealers as the "no see" cars, because they never seemed to meet their repeatedly rescheduled production dates—finally appeared in the spring of 1984.

CHAPTER NINE

1985 Coupe de Ville.

A Division in Limbo:
1985–91

THE NEW CADILLACS were dramatically different, of that there was no debate. Described in national advertising as "The Cadillac of Tomorrow," they featured front-drive technology, and a much smaller and more space-efficient package than any previous Cadillacs. Overall length had been reduced by 26 inches, the wheelbase by 10.5 inches, and 643 pounds had been shed with the high-volume Sedan de Ville. A glossy booklet prepared for Cadillac retail salesmen noted portentously, "This book is the most important selling guide in Cadillac history. That is because the new front-wheel-drive Cadillac Fleetwood, Coupe de Ville, and Sedan de Ville represent the direction of Cadillac's future. Further, that future is based on the sales successes of these new models." Alas, it was true.

In many respects, the coup de grace for Cadillac's image came in with these downsized front-drive DeVille/Fleetwood models. They had problems galore. One was the shabby build quality of early examples being shipped from the new plant in Lake Orion, Michigan. Originally conceived as Pontiac's new factory back before the reorganization when Pontiac was still in the car manufacturing business, it had been diverted to front-drive C-body production for Cadillac and the Olds 98. The early build quality, while troubling enough, was at least fixable. The design of the new cars was another matter.

General Motors had come under attack with the 1981–82 J-cars for their "me too" styling; it was next to impossible to tell any of the versions apart—from Chevy up through Cadillac—at any distance. The cycle was repeated with the A-cars that were announced a few months later. Fortune Magazine ran a devastating cover that illustrated four red A-cars from all participating divisions; they were indistinguishable. In the wake of the uproar resulting from that, Chairman Smith pledged General Motors would do better, but the C-cars fell into the same trap. Although not a single piece of exterior sheet-metal on the Cadillacs was shared with the Buick Electra or the Olds 98, they still looked like identical triplets. Clearly, there was a major design failure going on at the corporate level, but Cadillac paid a heavy price.

Worst of all, the front-drive Cadillac C-cars arrived just as the market for traditional-size luxury cars was rebounding. Ford, which simply did not have the money to develop a new Lincoln Town Car during this period, was forced to stick with its 1980-series product. That proved to be a gold mine for Lincoln when the big car boom returned almost concurrently with the introduction of the new C-body. In addition, a pleasant face-lift of the Town Car in 1985 smoothed out most of the awkward lines in the 1980 design.

Moreover, the Town Car's face-lift was magnificently timed because of Cadillac's disastrous decision to completely phase-out its rear-drive models. The old, full-size C-body Fleetwoods, redesignated the D-body Fleetwood Broughams, were slated to continue in production at least through 1985 before being scrapped, but were almost completely ignored by the division. While tens of millions were spent promoting the new front-drivers, the entire national advertising campaign for the Brougham consisted of exactly one magazine ad. With unintentional perceptiveness, the ad was headlined, "for all the reasons you have always owned a Cadillac." It could have been Lincoln's slogan for the Town Car, and many long-time Cadillac buyers switched over to Lincoln in the mistaken belief that Cadillac no longer offered a traditional-size luxury sedan. Largely as a consequence, Town Car production soared to 119,878 in 1985 (up from a pathetic 32,839 as recently as 1981). By 1988, overall Lincoln production would reach 280,659 units, 72 percent of them Town Cars, and Cadillac was in the toughest fight it had known in half-a-century.

In its determination to drive the point home, Lincoln managed to score a major coup with one of the most talked about television commercials of the era, a rare example of "attack" advertising that really worked. The commercial showed an elegant couple leaving a posh restaurant. They ask the valet for their Cadillac, only to be offered a look-alike Olds 98 that another elegantly dressed couple then confuses for their Buick, and so on, until a Lincoln Town

Car pulls up and yet another elegant couple gets in, obviously proud of their truly distinguished automobile. This commercial was devastatingly effective and it quickly achieved critical mass, i.e., it took on a life of its own and became part of the popular culture. Everyone from stand-up comedians to comic strip artists did take-offs. Needless to say, this did Cadillac no good at all in a market segment where distinction has always been one of the main buying motivations, while, at the same time positioning the Town Car as a non-look-alike alternative.

Lincoln made further significant headway with its limousine conversions in a market suddenly thrown wide open by a related strategic mistake at Cadillac. When the front-drive DeVille/Fleetwood series was announced, the stretched derivative of the rear-drive Brougham—the traditional Cadillac factory-built limousine—was dropped. To replace it, Cadillac struck a deal with the Hess and Eisenhardt to build limousines on the new DeVille platform. This program was an abject failure. The front-drive DeVille was too small for truly acceptable limousine application and independent converters—who supplied most of the stretched vehicles to the professional car industry by that time—hated working with the C-car's frameless unibody. Lincoln rushed in to capitalize on this opportunity, and a market that for decades had been virtually a Cadillac monopoly saw sudden and dramatic shift toward Lincoln as the dominant player. The numbers involved were not great—several thousand units

1985 Fleetwood Seventy-Five formal limousine in China.

per year, at most—but the prestige accruing to the dominant limousine manufacturer was (and is) enormous and Lincoln benefited accordingly.

As if anyone was paying much attention, the Cimarron came in for its first
major restyle in 1985. It consisted almost entirely of plastic add-on exterior
trim pieces. The Cavalier body and instrument panel were hardly touched. A
V6 engine option was, however, listed and offered the first (and only) non-
run-of-the-mill J-car option of any significance in the Cimarron's career. In
V6 form with an automatic transmission, the Cimarron was actually a fairly
pleasant little car, although still desperately lacking in Cadillac style or distinction. A total of 18,990 were built during the 1985 model run.

Except for an attractive new cast wheel option, there were virtually no
changes to the 1985 carry-over Seville and Eldorado models. They were due
for a completely new design for the 1986 model year, and therein loomed yet
another disaster for Cadillac.[1]

The same type of down-sizing done to the C-body cars in 1985 was done to
the Eldorado and Seville for 1986—and with much the same results. The 1986
"E/K" personal luxury cars (Buick Riviera, Olds Toronado, and Cadillac El-
dorado/Seville), in general, were tremendous disappointments for GM, both
aesthetically and commercially.

What appalled industry observers most about these cars was their near total
lack of distinction, a failing which has to be a capital crime in the luxury-
personal-car segment. When this writer attended the press launch of the 1986
Seville/Eldorado at Laguna Niguel, California, in the summer of 1985, Charles
M. "Chuck" Jordan, then General Motors' vice-president in charge of the De-

1985 Cimarron.

sign Staff, insisted in a conversation that these cars would grow on people and come to be regarded as having a "classic beauty" akin to the 1963 Riviera. At the time, it seemed like a put-on.[2]

The 1986 Seville and Eldorado were the archetypical dates with nice personalities. Looks aside, they were pleasant cars. They did the basic things a personal luxury car was supposed to do and did them fairly well, although they were nearly devoid of the kind of solid "road feel" and handling that younger luxury car buyers were starting to demand, and which the European competition was offering in abundance.

Again, Lincoln was the American manufacturer to really score in this emerging international-size segment with its remarkable Mark VII LSC introduced in 1984. The LSC was the "hot rod" Lincoln reborn—certainly as it had been developed by 1986—and perfectly embodied the blending of European size and appointments with the "baby boomer" approach to handling and performance. In stark contrast to the 1986 Seville and Eldorado, the Mark VII LSC was a revelation.

Even more worrisome, luxury cars from overseas were coming to be considered the prestige standards by many. By 1985, Mercedes-Benz and BMW, between them, had made German quality and performance the benchmarks in the luxury field with increasing numbers of buyers. Mercedes-Benz, in particular, had moved above Cadillac in price, as well, and was rapidly exploiting a new "ultra" luxury market for which General Motors had no competitor at all. Jaguar, once given up for dead, had used a combination of sex appeal and old-world craftsmanship to carve out a growing niche for the British end of the market. Perhaps most alarming of all, the Japanese manufacturers—renowned for both high quality products and a ferocious, take-no-prisoners aggressiveness in promoting them—were rumored to be preparing billion-dollar assaults of their own in the luxury market over the next several years. Indeed, the first wave of the assault, the Acura, had already arrived and was doing extremely well in its first season.

And, again, quality control problems plagued early examples of the E/K series. The cars were built in yet another new facility, this one in Hamtramck, a Detroit suburb.[3] Specifically constructed to build world-class quality, Hamtramck, in painful ways, became a metaphor for Chairman Roger Smith's "new" General Motors. He expected to use high-tech robotics to reduce the corporation's costs and improve its quality, but, instead, the plant quickly turned into a disaster area. The automated paint booth melted the plastic taillights on cars being painted. The robots that were supposed to flawlessly install windshields did not recognize certain paint colors and would send wind-

1985 Eldorado convertible.

shields smashing into cars. Many of the extravagantly expensive devices did not work at all—which may have been a blessing considering the mayhem caused by some of those that did. The myriad problems took years to sort out.

Hamtramck might have been an even worse disaster if customers had been lined-up waiting for the new Eldorados and Sevilles. They were not. Eldorado demand was down by a startling 72 percent for the model run. The Seville, which had never really caught on with luxury car buyers after its razorback redo in 1980, slid a mere 52 percent. It was a catastrophe that extended to the similarly unappealing Riviera and Toronado lines, as well. Moreover, these were high margin cars for all the divisions involved and for their dealers. General Motors alone reportedly lost $500 million a year due to the collapse in sales.

For Cadillac, the Eldorado/Seville fiasco was the final straw. Coming on top of the front-drive C-car fiasco of the previous year, and everything else that had gone before in the terrible 1980s, it was obvious even to those in the division that something was desperately wrong. Goodness knows, it was obvious to the press corps. One of the major automotive magazines ran a cover story in November, 1986, entitled, "The Decline and Fall of Cadillac," which must have sent shivers up the spines of many on Clark Street—and "downtown," as well.[4]

Most significantly of all, it was obvious to Bill Hoglund, who was named group vice-president in charge of the Buick-Olds-Cadillac Group at about this time. Hoglund had something of a reputation at General Motors: 1) for being outspoken, and 2) for being just about the smartest marketing man in the company. It had been Hoglund who had taken over at Pontiac when that division seemed to be going down for the count, developed the "excitement" image and the cars to go with it, and turned Pontiac into the corporation's raging success story of the 1980s. The key to Hoglund's achievement at Pontiac had been defining the division's image, and then getting everyone to act accordingly. It seems an obvious thing in retrospect, but Pontiac had lost its way. Part of the division's problems had been due to external factors that had whipsawed it this way and that during the 1970s. Hoglund recalled:

> In ten years we had four general managers, each of them struggling to find the right direction for Pontiac based on the changing external factors in '70s. Fuel got to be a problem, and then fuel's not a problem, then price is a problem.[5]

As Hoglund came to see it, the fundamental problem at Pontiac had been the way in which those problems had been met. The division had trapped itself in a no-win game of trying to satisfy the constantly fluctuating market demands of the moment. John Middlebrook, then a product planner at Pontiac and now vice president for GM, summarizes the type of thinking:

> Why is Olds selling all those Cutlass Supremes? Let's get a car like that. Why is Buick doing better up here? Let's put some velour trim in. I saw it in those years as trying to be all things to all people.[6]

Clearly, by 1986, Cadillac was deeply mired in the same quagmire. Warren D. Hirschfield, who had spent his career at Cadillac and been named chief engineer about the time of the reorganization, put his finger on the problem in an interview given at the time:

> We've got this Sears thing. "This is our regular, this is our better, this is our best." We've got to stop that.[7]

1985 Fleetwood.

1986 Cimarron D'Oro.

Hoglund had every intention of making sure they did. The lack of product focus at Cadillac was only one nagging problem he saw, though. Even more disturbing to him was the fact that Mercedes-Benz (and other European brands) had been allowed to open up a lucrative high-end luxury segment uncontested by General Motors. Mercedes-Benz S-Class prices started at $47,700. The priciest standard Cadillac, carried a base sticker of $26,756. Worse, the Coupe de Ville actually listed for less than the Buick Riviera. The luxury market was moving upscale and Cadillac was not moving with it. As Hoglund dryly noted, "Cadillac was coming down on top of Buick." He continued:

> When I got to B-O-C, I talked to Grettenberger about that. I had told the
> organization that there is need to have Cadillac the best car in the world.
> We've already got a second best car in the world, and that's Buick. If you guys
> aren't clearly up there fighting with Mercedes and BMW, what do we need
> you for? You're just a drain. You can't command any more price. You get
> $20,000, Mercedes gets $40,000![8]

The mission for Grettenberger was clear: find a way to make Cadillac a top contender by world standards. Grettenberger would spend the remainder of his lengthy tenure at Cadillac doing just that.

None of the foregoing should be taken to suggest that Grettenberger was unaware of the need to move Cadillac up-market to compete effectively against the European luxury producers with the new kind of Cadillac Hoglund wanted. He was, and had been actively pursuing plans—including the forthcoming Allanté—to do just that. The main difference was targeting. Grettenberger wanted to cover the entire market from near luxury (Cimarron) to standard luxury (DeVille and Fleetwood) to ultra luxury (Mercedes-

Benz, et. al.). Hoglund believed that such a broad approach would work against corporate interests by keeping Cadillac in head-to-head competition with Buick on the low end, and, at the same time, work against Cadillac's own interests by keeping the division from focusing on its true mission: certifiable, world-class luxury cars. In particular, Hoglund was having trouble working out a viable market positioning for Buick, another problem division at that time. Having Cadillac stomping around on Buick's turf was not the way to help the cause, in Hoglund's view, particularly considering that Buick and Olds had given up resources to aid in the emergency restyling Cadillac needed to fund for the 1988 Eldorado, 1989 DeVille/Fleetwood lines, and—looking several years into the future—the 1992 Eldorado/Seville. This is how matters finally came to a head according to Hoglund:

> We had to twist their arms to get them to drop the Cimarron...[At that time] we worked as a group staff trying to position Buick. We thought we were going to have no trouble positioning them quite easily, but they all gave up resources to Cadillac so Cadillac could do the '89, so they could get the four-five [the 4.5 liter engine] and then the four-nine out, so they could get on with the Seville/Eldorado that is coming out this year [1991 as 1992 models]. So, we were having a meeting on forward strategy at one point—and I'm sticking this market differentiation together—and so I said, "John [Grettenberger], I talked to you about six months ago about the Cimarron. Is the Cimarron consistent with your market direction?" And, he said, "No. But it's worth 20,000 cars." "So, I'll make a deal with you. These guys—Oldsmobile and Buick—have given up resources for you to sell the best car in the world, or set the direction to get there. The deal I have is that if they support you I'll let you keep the Cimarron. But, if they don't support you, you've got to cut the Cimarron." And, I hadn't talked to anybody. So, of ten guys we had who were on the group staff we had a closed vote, and the score was nine to one. So, he dropped it.[9]

1986 DeVille Touring Coupe.

The Cimarron would linger through the 1988 model year, but then Cadillac would be out of the near-luxury segment for good. In the meantime, Grettenberger and his staff had been hard at work dealing with the shortcomings in the other product lines he had inherited. Customers had complained about the dreadfully plain looks of the 1985 DeVille models, so for 1986 they had been upgraded with Fleetwood exterior trim. The enthusiast magazines had complained about the lack of European character in the same models, so for 1986 mid-year DeVille Touring Edition models were announced that featured monochromatic trim and major suspension recalibrations. Everyone had complained about the size of the new DeVilles and Fleetwoods, particularly in comparison to the full-size Lincolns, so for 1987 the front-drive models were lengthened slightly and a limited-edition, long-wheelbase Sixty Special was added to the line.

The restyling of the DeVilles and Fleetwoods had been accomplished almost entirely by refashioning the rear fender caps, but the result was quite pleasing and did a lot to dress-up the models affected. The Sixty Special, on the other hand, which consisted of a five-inch stretch to the rear passenger compartment and a daunting $34,850 price tag, was not intended as a volume product line. Converted from the standard Fleetwood by Hess and Eisenhardt—possibly in an effort to use up plant space made available by the slow-selling front-drive limousines—it was more a statement of Cadillac's future direction. In that, it forecast the 1989 C-body redesign then in the works.

1986 Seville Eleganté.

The division also began hiking its prices in 1987. Hoglund had told them to build $40,000 cars or else and they, apparently, determined that one way to do that was to raise their prices. Clearly, a $20,000 price jump would have spelled disaster, but small increases over a period of several years would accomplish the same purpose in time. In the decade following 1986, the base price of the DeVille went from just under $20,000 to $35,995—an increase of around 68 percent, which represented far more than inflationary pressure. High-end Cadillacs topped even that and approached $50,000 for the Seville STS.

The big splash for Cadillac in 1987, however, was the Allanté. The project had originated back in 1982 at about the time Bob Burger became general

Top, 1986 Eldorado Biarritz interior; *bottom*, 1986 Eldorado.

1986 Sedan DeVille.

manager. The point man and team leader was Warren Hirschfield. What the division was looking for was a high-profile image car that would announce to the world that Cadillac was moving up—specifically, to stake out Cadillac's presence in the new ultra luxury market being exploited by the Europeans. General Motors' normal design and engineering channels were avoided, presumably to keep the car from being bogged down in the corporate committee system.

Pininfarina in Italy was selected for the job. The last true Cadillac customs, the Eldorado Broughams of 1959 and 1960, had also been Pininfarina-built. Since then, Pininfarina had created some of the most acclaimed European automotive designs, including those for nearly all the modern Ferraris. In its essentials, the Allanté was a co-operative venture between Cadillac and Pininfarina.

The idea behind the Allanté project was to create a blend between the best of European design and coachbuilding with the best of American engineering. To that end, the Allanté was entirely designed by Pininfarina (under Cadillac supervision), and the Allanté body was completely manufactured and finished in a new Pininfarina plant in Turin, Italy, constructed just for that purpose. The bodies were then flown (that's right, flown) in specially rigged 747s on an "air bridge" from Turin to Detroit, where they were mated to specially designed Cadillac engines and running gear at the Hamtramck plant. Cadillac went so far as to build a small Allanté test track next to the plant where every Allanté was road tested for 25 miles before shipment to the dealer. This operation involved the full attention of no less than two—count them, two—white-smocked Allanté inspectors.

Styling is inevitably the most subjective aspect of a car. The Allanté was not

1987 Allanté: *top*, the "air bridge"; *middle*, interior; *bottom*, exterior.

knock-your-socks-off beautiful in the manner of a Ferrari Testarossa, but even its detractors, for the most part, agreed it was good-looking. It was a clean, unified, thoroughly handsome design. Basically a convertible, it also came, at least initially, with a detachable hardtop that turned it into an all-weather coupe. (Later, the hardtop was relegated to the options list in order to bring the Allanté's base price down.)

In general, the Allanté's interior was superb. A big surprise was the amount of interior room; two-seater convertibles had come a long way from the British variety common in the 1950s. The trunk, too, was surprisingly large. In size and feel, the Allanté was much more a luxury car than a typical sports car.

Under the skin, the Allanté shared its front-wheel drive basics with other Cadillacs, but the 4.1 liter V8 was specially reworked with electronic sequential-port fuel injection, delivered 170 horsepower (30 more than the DeVille), and was, in that version, unique to the Allanté. The Allanté version also featured an aluminum cylinder block for weight reduction with cast iron cylinder liners and heads. Anti-lock brakes, fully-independent suspension is at all four corners, and unique Goodyear Eagle "VL" tires rounded out the package. The Allanté handled superbly, perhaps better than any car in its league, lacking only gut-wrenching acceleration to be a world-beater.

Cadillac had promised to introduce the Allanté at a price point under $50,000 and, in fact, at least one of the enthusiast magazines officially listed it at $49,000. Alas, it was not to be. When the Allanté finally arrived in dealer showrooms, the sticker said $54,700, which struck a lot of people as a lot of money. Inevitably, many prospects saw the sticker and said, "$54,700 for a Cadillac?!"

Cadillac planners had apparently sold the project to corporate management—and, ultimately, to the nation's auto writers—on the basis of a projected 7,000–8,000 sales per year. As it turned out, demand was about half that and unsold Allantés soon began piling up at the factory. A total of 4,718 were built during the 1987 model run, but only 2,517 actually found buyers during the calendar year. Sales did begin to show modest gains after that, but never came close to meeting the targets originally set.

What happened? One problem with the Allanté had been the over-expectations General Motors had for it before it was announced to the public. The market for such cars was not large and, perhaps critically, Cadillac had no reputation in it or at anything like that price level. The division might have licked its wounds and elected to content itself with the 3,000 or so Allantés for which a market actually existed, but there was a larger problem.

Simply put, Cadillac had at that time probably the worst relations with the

automotive press corps of any manufacturer. In the 1980s, as the division's fortunes deteriorated, the traditional aloofness of the public relations department
had descended into a pervasive suspicion and hostility toward the nation's automotive writers, who were seen as somehow responsible for Cadillac's decline.
At its worst, this attitude was manifested in ham-handed attempts to manage
the news. The most pedestrian requests for press kits, photos, or production
figures were often met with an icy, "What do you want that for?" AutoWeek
magazine noted in 1986 that the division's public relations department "hear-
kens to a dark age of parochialism and arrogance" and, by 1987, there were
mounting concerns at the corporate level. These concerns were hardly assuaged
when the noted auto writer for the Chicago Sun-Times published a blistering
ad hominem attack on Cadillac's public relations director. Such actions on the
part of the automotive press corps were absolutely unprecedented, and according to a highly placed source in General Motors, prompted a determined
effort within the Buick-Olds-Cadillac Group to force Grettenberger to under-
take a thorough housecleaning. Grettenberger, reportedly, refused.

Press relations are not terribly tricky when a car company is doing well.
When a company really needs a friendly—or, at least, not openly hostile—
press corps is when things are going as badly, as they were for Cadillac in the
middle of the 1980s. It was rumored, that several of the important enthusiast
magazines had gotten to the point where they actively searched for negative
things to publish about Cadillacs and about the division. There was certainly
no obvious inclination on the part of the mass of the nation's auto writers to
give the division a pass on anything. So, when Allanté sales failed to take off,
as the division had confidently—and perhaps rashly—predicted, the knives
came out. Overnight, the Allanté became the "big flop" story of the year in
magazines and newspapers from coast-to-coast. The damage done was substantial and, quite possibly, fatal. Once branded a loser, the Allanté became
one—dealers lost faith, customers began shying away, and the program was
sent into a downward spiral from which it arguably never recovered.[10]

Overall, Cadillac calendar production declined 14 percent from 1986 as the
Eldorado and Seville continued to slide. Worse, Lincoln was gaining strength
—Cadillac's four-to-one lead at the start of the decade had been shaved to
three-to-two—and Lincoln had an important new model announcement in
the wings for 1988. Jaguar had already made a major product launch with its all-
new XJ6 range in 1987. Mercedes-Benz had introduced a successful 300-Class
mid-range car just prior to that, while the new BMW 5-Series was slated to follow in 1989. The competition, it seemed, was no more inclined to give Cadillac
a pass than were the nation's auto writers.

The year was not an unmitigated disaster for Cadillac, however. Perhaps Grettenberger's most critically important single achievement during his entire tenure at Cadillac's helm was recorded in January, 1987. At that time, Cadillac officially succeeded in reversing the reorganization of 1984. Cadillac regained control of most of its old functions and took exclusive dominion over the spanking new plant at Hamtramck. The corporation's deepening fear for

Top, 1988 Eldorado; *bottom*, 1988 4.5-liter engine.

the division's future was a key element in the astounding decision, and it was a victory with long-term implications. Once again, the division was a cohesive car company able to design, engineer, manufacture, and sell its own products. The division was going to need every break it could get.

For 1988, an Allanté buyer could have a choice of digital and analog gauges. The digital cluster—a multi-hued, Tokyo-by-night, electronic extravaganza—had been standard in 1987, but most enthusiasts preferred the low-tech analogs. Most enthusiasts wanted more power in the Allanté, as well, so the engine was increased in displacement to 4.5 liters. In addition, a detuned version of this 4.5 liter powerplant was standard across the board in all Cadillac models except the rear-drive Brougham. The downside was that torque steer, the bane of front-drive technology, appeared with the power increase. Still, the division was trying.

More importantly, the Eldorado received its emergency restyling for 1988. New quarter panels all around and some creative trim modifications resulted in a car that was a significant improvement over the previous model, although hardly the complete transformation that was needed. Sales, nevertheless, turned upward at last. A reasonably satisfying 33,210 were built during the model run. This was a far cry from the good old days, but nearly double the disastrous pace of 1987.

The Seville was more modestly reworked to try to render it at least marginally competitive. It was still an example of trying to make a silk purse out of a sow's ear; Cadillac designers and engineers didn't have much to work with, but sales still rose about 25 percent. The most interesting result of the effort to resuscitate the Seville came in mid-year with the announcement of the Seville STS high performance sedan. With its touring suspension and beautiful, elm wood burl interior trim, the Seville had at last been upgraded sufficiently to compete credibly against low-end Mercedes and BMW models. Cadillac was learning to listen to its customers and the Seville STS was critically important in pointing the future direction of Cadillac product design. More would be heard about this model later, but, in the meantime, Lincoln would demonstrate just how important the Seville's market segment was becoming.

The big story at Lincoln in 1988 was the completely redesigned Continental. Based on Ford's wildly successful Taurus/Sable platform, the new Continental was a big hit, too. In fact, sales consistently outran production throughout the model year, the first time in many a year Ford had faced that problem with a Lincoln series (and it must have brought back tender memories on Clark Street, too). The Continental was immediately perceived as the leader in the small luxury sedan market, with sales that nearly doubled the reworked Seville, even given Lincoln's capacity restraints at the time.

Technically, Lincoln actually out-produced Cadillac overall in the 1988 model run. This was achieved through a bit of a dirty trick, though. Lincoln ended its 1987 model production early in 1987 and then had a year-and-a-half with the 1988s. Still, for the 1988 calendar year, Lincoln closed the gap significantly, reaching 78 percent of Cadillac production.

The more imposing size of the Sixty Special was carried to the entire front-drive sedan range for 1989, in the first major overhaul of those models since their introduction in the spring of 1984. Gone was the semi-custom Sixty Special, replaced by a new standard 113.8-inch wheelbase for all sedans, including Sedan de Ville and Fleetwood/Fleetwood Sixty Special. Equally important from a marketing standpoint, overall length was increased by 8 inches. The Coupe de Ville remained at the old size, which was fine for two reasons: 1) the

Top, 1989 Sedan DeVille; *bottom*, 1989 Fleetwood.

two-door body style looked sportier on the shorter length, and 2) sales of this configuration had been abysmal for Olds, Buick, and Cadillac alike. The market was clearly shifting to four doors with full-size luxury cars, and the Sedan de Ville was the urgent problem if Cadillac was to fend off the growing challenge from Lincoln.

For years, Cadillac officials had been earnestly hoping that the old rear-drive Brougham would simply go away. The distaste that Cadillac—and, significantly, General Motors executives—held for the rear-drive models in these years should not be understated. Chairman Roger Smith and Bob Stempel, who had been elevated to the presidency in 1987, positively loathed rear-drive technology. In a 1991 interview conducted after he had risen to chairman, Stempel stated flatly, "There are some corporate things we're going to drive; we are a front-drive corporation." Stempel admitted that the then-new 1992 Buick Roadmaster and Chevrolet Caprice rear-drive lines had been put into production "over my dead body." The paying customers, however, refused to be dissuaded.

General Motors wanted front-drive, unibody technology for manufacturing reasons, primarily. Such cars were easier and cheaper to build, and, therefore, were an asset in the corporation's obsession to make its assembly operations more efficient. This was a legitimate goal, since General Motors was still the highest-cost producer in the American industry despite the reported $50 billion Smith had thrown at the problem through new plant construction, automation, and robotics. There were, however, problems with this strategy insofar as Cadillac was concerned. Front-drive induced torque steer in the high-output engines Cadillac was forced to use to remain competitive. The unibody was difficult to engineer with high standards of road isolation. By comparison, the "old technology" Town Car was a far more pleasant driving car—at least in a straight line—and silent as a tomb.

Remarkably, after years of being willfully ignored in both promotion and meaningful product development, the rear-drive Brougham still accounted for nearly one-in-five full-size Cadillac sales. The 1989 DeVille/Fleetwood restyle made some headway, though, at least temporarily. Front-drive Cadillac production rose by 17 percent, while Lincoln Town Car production plummeted. It was the calm before the storm, however, since Lincoln was about to introduce a dramatically revised Town Car for the 1990 model year that would redefine the luxury market. As if that weren't enough, there was a looming threat from across the sea that posed an even more daunting challenge.[11]

A major assist to Lincoln's growth was provided by aggressive development work done by Ford Motor Company's Limousine and Police Vehicles Product

1990 Seville STS.

Development staff, beginning around this time. Observing the growing Lincoln popularity among the conversion companies and concerned about the fairly slipshod engineering in evidence in all-too-many cases, Ford instituted an aggressive program to work directly with converters to improve their products, regardless of the chassis used (although their most detailed technical support naturally involved Lincoln). At first, the converters were suspicious—to say nothing of Ford's counterparts at Cadillac—but this program did so much to raise the quality level of the entire conversion industry that even Cadillac finally saw the light and belatedly inaugurated a similar program of its own.

For the 1990 model year, the Allanté, then entering its fourth season, remained essentially unchanged except for the addition of "traction control" as standard equipment. In this development, Cadillac blazed an important technological trail. Traction control was the logical next step following the advent of anti-lock braking (ABS) on the Allanté in 1987. ABS, one of the greatest safety advances since hydraulic brakes, controls the stopping power to a car's wheels during braking in order to prevent wheel lock-up and, with it, skidding. Traction control was designed to do the same thing for acceleration. Lexus (of whom more will be heard shortly) also offered a similar system as an option, and other manufacturers were destined to follow suit in short order. Once again, though, Cadillac was an industry leader with a truly important engineering advance.

The successful Seville STS, also designed to counter the European threat— and doing a much better job of it—continued to shore-up Cadillac's flank in that direction. For 1990, it was joined by a similar Eldorado Touring Coupe model.

Cadillac also bowed to the inevitable and spruced up the rear-drive Broug-ham for the first time in years. Although a major overhaul of the aging rear-drive model was still a couple of years away, it received a substantial freshen-ing in hopes of keeping it competitive against the all-new Lincoln Town Car. New body side moldings brought Brougham styling into line with the current Cadillac "look," while halogen headlamps, anti-lock brakes, and the optional General Motors 5.7 liter V8 were important technical improvements. The 5.7 liter engine was the largest in the General Motors passenger car arsenal.

Despite Cadillac's exertions, Lincoln scored a direct hit—strategically and commercially—with its completely redesigned 1990 Town Car. Armed with the knowledge that the "baby boom" generation was inevitably becoming older and more affluent, Lincoln sought to create a luxury car that would maintain the Town Car's enviable reputation for size and luxury, yet add to it more youthful attributes sure to be valued by the next generation of luxury car buyers, such as efficiency, performance, and handling. The 1990 Town Car, for example, had a shape that was much more aerodynamic than its predecessor and even utilized exotic design tricks, such as flush-mounted side window glass. Fuel economy was significantly improved as a result, as was the reduction in wind noise. The 1990 Town Car was so silent at highway speeds it practically redefined the term, and it got even quieter in 1991 with the ad-vent of the 4.6 liter "modular" V8. Suspension modifications also improved the Town Car's stability, particularly on poor roads.

Largely on the strength of the Town Car's soaring popularity, Lincoln shaved

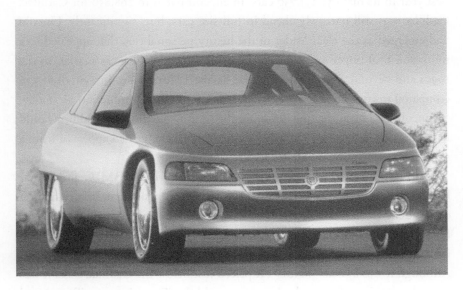

1990 Aurora concept car.

Top, 1991 Brougham; *bottom*, 1991 Sedan DeVille.

Cadillac's once untouchable lead in sales of only a few years earlier from a margin of three-to-one to near parity. In June of 1990, Lincoln nearly out-sold Cadillac nationally for the first time in history. Lincoln ended with the second best year in its history: 233,730 cars, in all, compared to 268,850 for Cadillac. Cadillac was still narrowly ahead in full-size cars, but, significantly, Lincoln had emerged as the clear leader in the luxury personal cars that appealed to a more youthful buyer and forecast the future of the luxury car market in the 1990s and beyond. Combined Cadillac Seville/Eldorado production of 57,376 compared to combined Lincoln Mark VII/Continental production of 76,687. If Lincoln had been the only looming threat in 1990, though, Cadillac would have counted itself lucky. Unfortunately, a new challenge had appeared from a source not previously known for luxury cars.

During the 1980s, Europeans such as Mercedes-Benz, BMW, and Jaguar had transformed themselves from curiosities into mainstream luxury market contenders. In the fall of 1989, the Japanese joined the fray with a serious effort of their own designed to crack the upscale market. The threat had been coming for several years. The Acura had first appeared from Honda in 1986. Although it was a "near" luxury car priced just below the Cadillac class, it was an early warning of what the Japanese could do. Then, in 1990, Toyota and

Nissan fielded new luxury nameplates—Lexus and Infiniti, respectively—that offered carefully thought-out, broad-based challenges not only to Cadillac and Lincoln, but to the well-entrenched Europeans, as well.

For Cadillac, the Japanese posed a particularly unsettling threat. There were millions of Americans who had, for years, driven nothing but Japanese cars. A large percentage of them were "baby boomers" in the highly prized thirty-five to forty-five-year-old age bracket. The Acura, Lexus, and Infiniti were, in part, a defensive effort by the Japanese to keep these customers in the fold as they grew older and more affluent—in other words, for the same reason Ford Motor Company was so intent upon developing the Lincoln as a credible luxury-brand alternative in the 1950s. But, part of the strategy behind them was an aggressive effort to carve out a lucrative new presence at the expense of the entrenched competition. Cadillac (and Lincoln, too) realized that, by 1995, this demographic group would begin to exert tremendous influence on the luxury car market and, if they retained their Japanese buying habits, it could spell real trouble.

Cadillac's major product news for 1991—a new 4.9 liter V8 engine for its most popular models—was hardly sufficient to stem the tide. With the nightmare of the 1980s concluded, Grettenberger and his associates recognized that the coming decade of the 1990s would be the make-or-break years for Cadillac. Their solution was a whole new generation of Cadillac products being prepared for introduction to the market beginning in the 1992 model year. They understood that the success of these new products would probably determine the future of the division well into the 21st century—would, in fact, determine if the division had a future at all.

Grettenberger stated the division's goals this way:

> Cadillacs must be exclusive and distinctive. We have to stand out from our
> competition, whether it be other General Motors products or those from
> other manufacturers. As long as we are the flagship division of General
> Motors, you can bet that we will offer the very top in terms of exclusivity
> and modern, leading-edge features and technology.[12]

Brave words. But, Cadillac's future, depended upon Grettenberger being right, for nothing less was going to suffice to keep Cadillac at the top of the pack in the fiercely competitive luxury market.

CHAPTER TEN

Cadillac Evoq concept car.

Cadillac Fights Back:
1992–01

BY THE TIME the 1960s came along, with all its foes vanquished, it seemed as if Cadillac had achieved uncontested leadership in the luxury field. Over the years, Cadillac had beaten the best this country could produce. Legendary makes such as Packard, Pierce-Arrow, Marmon, Franklin, Duesenberg, Cord, and Stutz, one by one, slid into oblivion while the Colossus of Clark Street sailed on.

Yet, the market, like nature, abhors a vacuum and new challengers appeared. This time, and for the first time, some of the principal challengers came from other shores. Partly as a result of that, and partly as a result of massive international economic disruptions in the 1970s, Cadillac found itself in the toughest fight of its existence in the 1980s. The luxury market was being redefined yet again, only this time, those guiding the division's fortunes failed to see the change coming, and once it had come, failed to take decisive steps to remold Cadillac to the new reality.

In retrospect, perhaps the most important single event in the modern history of the luxury car field occurred in 1958 when Ford invented the four-seater Thunderbird. The first of what came to be known as "personal luxury" cars, the Thunderbird was built with a shape that was sleek, incredibly low by the standards of the day, and designed to carry only four people—five, if the three in the back were very good friends (or wanted to be). Moreover, the front passengers sat in individual bucket seats separated by a console. The Thunderbird was the first successful luxury car in modern times to suggest that quality could be measured by something other than the cubic yard—a radical notion, indeed, in the 1950s. It wasn't long before General Motors followed with models of its own: the classically good-looking Buick Riviera in 1963, then the Oldsmobile Toronado in 1966, and, finally, the Cadillac Eldorado in 1967. Lincoln weighed-in with the Mark III series in 1968. They were not alone.

Across the water, Europeans had been building small luxury cars for years. European tax laws, traffic conditions and fuel prices all demanded them. Still, European luxury cars of the time were really too small for mass-American tastes in the expansive 1950s and 1960s. Even cars of the four-seater T-Bird genre, while trending in the right direction, were huge and monstrously inefficient by prevailing European standards. Then came the 1970s and a number of factors interacted to progressively merge the European and American concepts, and accelerate the trend toward a common international luxury car type.

Increasing affluence in Europe caused luxury car buyers over there to demand greater size, comfort and power. Here in America, the fuel scares of 1973 and 1979 brought about a fundamental rethinking of efficiency standards, while the growing importance of the "baby boom" generation—a demographic group weaned on the high performance and sporty cars of the 1960s (Mustangs, GTOs, etc.)—prompted greater attention to non-traditional luxury car traits such as handling and performance. As a result of all these factors, European luxury rigs such as Mercedes-Benz got bigger and fancier, while American luxury car manufacturers—i.e., Cadillac and Lincoln—began to offer more efficiently-sized and sportier vehicles of their own. Still, the domestic manufacturers were slow to appreciate the shift in this growing segment and the potential for lush profits it offered, and their early efforts were hesitant.

Cadillac was the first to seem to appreciate the challenge and its initial effort was promising. The 1976 Seville was well conceived, solidly successful, and even had a modicum of success in European markets. The next generation of the Seville, introduced in 1980 (and the related Eldorado, introduced in 1979), however, failed to build on that initial success, while the third generation, introduced for the 1986 model year for both Seville and Eldorado, was calamitous and represented the low point of Cadillac's near-collapse as a serious luxury car producer in the 1980s. Moreover, they came hard on the heels of the disastrous C-bodied DeVilles and Fleetwoods of the previous year, and followed a disheartening trail of failures throughout the early years of the decade.

Lincoln, with far less in the way of resources at its disposal than Cadillac, was nevertheless the American manufacturer to show the way toward the emerging international-size segment, although it took two misfires to hit the target. Lincoln rushed its compact Versailles to completion in the spring of 1977 in what turned out to be a major failure in "packaging" (to borrow a bit of design jargon). The successor to the Versailles, the compact Continental introduced in 1982, was far better, but never made much of an impression on the market. Lincoln's first real success was with its remarkable Mark VII LSC introduced in 1984, a car that was years ahead of its time and that perfectly embodied the blending of European size and appointments with the "baby boomer" approach to handling and performance. The Mark VII LSC was also the clearest indication up to that time of the dramatic improvements Ford was making in building world-class quality. Both were lessons that Cadillac would fail to learn at its peril.

As the 1980s drew on, Jaguar, Mercedes-Benz, and BMW all moved aggressively to solidify their holds on a significant segment of the American luxury car buyers with precisely these kinds of cars. Still, the truly momentous news came in the latter part of the 1980s, when the Japanese entered the fray with highly competitive models of their own. The luxury class was the only market segment the Japanese had failed to crack and industry competitors—American and European alike—were bracing themselves for the onslaught. The Lexus LS 400 sedan (from Toyota) and the Infiniti Q45 sedan (from Nissan) were both announced in time for the 1990 model year. The Lexus, in par-

1992 Eldorado.

ticular, sent designers, engineers and marketing mavens at luxury car companies all over the world rushing back to their drawing boards. The sporty Lexus SC400 coupe followed in 1991 and continues to add luster to the growing Lexus reputation.

Suddenly, a type of luxury car that did not even exist twenty years before had developed into the fastest growing, and most hotly contested, part of the luxury market. Any manufacturer that wanted to be taken seriously as a luxury car producer in the 1990s knew it was going to have to be competitive in that segment. And, there was considerable question within the industry as to the ability of Cadillac, in particular, to make the grade—and, if it could not, what would it mean for the future of Cadillac as a viable nameplate?

The doubts and fears extended to the highest levels of General Motors. Cadillac's general manager, John O. Grettenberger, had been in no uncertain terms placed on notice that Cadillac had to go after this evolving international luxury car segment—or else. Cadillac engineers, designers and marketers were put to work developing their response to this life-or-death challenge. The result of that historic effort arrived in the fall of 1991: the 1992 Seville and Eldorado, arguably the most important new Cadillac models announced in a generation, if not in our lifetimes.

The 1992 Seville and Eldorado were developed from the previous Seville and Eldorado platforms, yet much work was done on them that they practically qualified as new-from-the-ground-up. Cadillac's long-awaited Northstar V8 engine failed to make it to production in time for their launch, though, so power came from the proven, 200 horsepower, 4.9 liter V8.

In the opinion of most design experts, exterior design remained one category in which the Japanese were clearly out in front. Nevertheless, the Seville, while very conservative in its basic design, was immediately regarded by many as perhaps the best-looking of the sedans in the new international class. The Seville STS differed in appearance from the standard edition mostly in terms of exterior ground effects. The Seville's attention to detail extended to its interior, where it offered a surprisingly pleasing blend of German and American design concepts. In the opinion of many reviewers, this impression was marred somewhat by use of too many off-the-shelf General Motors components, but it was otherwise regarded as perhaps the most pleasingly modern of the group.

The Seville and the Eldorado, on the other hand, suffered to some degree from less effective road isolation that made them noticeably noisier than they should have been. Cadillac ride quality was good, but a bit choppy by comparison with the best in this category.

The Eldorado was greeted less enthusiastically than the Seville. Its exterior styling was even less adventuresome than the Seville, and, in the opinion of most observers, not nearly as successful. The interior and chassis however were virtually identical.

Overall, most reviewers were of the opinion that Cadillac, while it did not score a knock out blow in the market segment, nonetheless proved it could mount a respectable challenge. Cadillac was clearly back in the game with Seville and Eldorado models that were fully competitive in most categories.

The Northstar engine, a state-of-the-art, 32-valve, overhead-cam V8, finally

Top, 1992 Seville STS interior; *bottom*, 1992 Seville STS.

1992 Seville.

appeared on the 1993 models. A head-to-head comparison between the Cadillac and Mercedes models was interesting, indeed, but no more so than my back-to-back evaluations of 1992 and 1993 Allanté models. The quietness, smoothness, power and general refinement of the Northstar engine were obvious from the moment you turned the key. In addition, in the process of re-engineering the Allanté engine bay to take the new V8, the front end was strengthened and stiffened in ways that made for a noticeably more solid car, and Allanté engineers did an impressive job in eliminating previous handling problems related to the Allanté's front-drive configuration.

Overall, the 1993 Allanté was the equal to the Mercedes 500SL in every important respect except complexity, heft and price. The 1993 Allanté listed for around $61,000. The 500SL carried a sticker of $99,000, a $38,000 difference that was pretty hard to explain in the Benz's favor by any objective standard. This two-way contest was never the blow-out in favor of the Germans that many industry observers thought it would be when Cadillac first announced its intention to enter the market back in the mid-1980s, and, with the addition of the Northstar V8 and the superior performance it provided, the Allanté finally became, objectively speaking, the best car in its class.

In my review of the original Allanté, I had noted:

> Cadillac is committed to the Allanté. They have no real choice. To pull back now would be to concede that Cadillac cannot make it head-to-head in the upper end of the market against Mercedes, BMW, Jaguar. They cannot afford to do that; there is simply too much at stake. So, they will just have to sort out their over-production problems in time and get on with the project on a more realistic basis.[1]

Alas, there was an unprecedented upheaval at General Motors in December, 1992. When the dust cleared, Chairman Robert Stempel was sacked along with much of the old guard and the corporation launched a draconian cost-cutting

CADILLAC

FIGHTS BACK

program. In a sense, it had no choice. It was losing billions. Unfortunately, one of the first victims of the new regime was the Allanté. In depressingly typical GM fashion, just when they had finally got the car right, they killed it.

For the 1993 model year, the really big push was the new rear-drive Cadillac Fleetwood. Tired (at long last!) of watching the Lincoln Town Car eat its lunch, Cadillac had decided to launch a counter-attack. The 1993 Fleetwood was big, which was probably its main selling point with the traditional Cadillac clientele. In fact, it was even bigger than the Buick Roadmaster (with which it shared General Motors' B-body platform), with a stretch of 6 inches in wheelbase and nearly 10 inches in overall length. Cadillac did a complete

Top, 1993 Fleetwood interior; *bottom*, 1993 Fleetwood.

1993 Northstar engine.

re-engineering of the platform along the way, and the Cadillac version seemed to be a beefier and altogether more imposing car. While much of this, no doubt, was due to styling tricks, it was a fact that the Fleetwood (with the optional towing package) carried an impressive 7,000-pound tow rating—the highest rating for an American passenger car.

The predecessor to the current limousine was a Fleetwood Brougham, delivered to the Clinton Administration in 1993. Unlike previous models, the Presidential Brougham was designed, developed and manufactured totally within General Motors. It was designed to minimize exposure to external threats, with neither sunroof nor running boards. The vehicle is still in service and was also used in the inaugural parade.

Since 1992, every Cadillac product line had been redone. For 1994, it was the turn of the volume DeVille line. The new DeVilles were a curious cross between the styling of the big, rear-drive Fleetwood sedan, with the size and performance of the Seville. In fact, the DeVille now used the same platform as the Seville and was built right alongside it in Cadillac's state-of-the-art plant at Hamtramck, Michigan. Early sales statistics showed them halting Lincoln's growth—and, just in the nick of time, too. Cadillac's lead over Lincoln, which stood at a ratio of 7 to 1 in 1960, was down to 6 to 5 in 1993. Lincoln clearly had the initiative among domestic luxury producers, and the foreign contenders showed no sign of easing the pressure, either.

Cadillac still sold more luxury cars than anyone in America, but the margin had steadily eroded in recent years under assaults both foreign and domestic, and the division was going to have to do some rather fancy work in the next few years to retain even its diminished position. There was serious discussion among industry observers regarding whether General Motors could move quickly enough in a ferociously competitive market to give luxury car buyers what they demanded.

Also, according to most observers, whatever chance the division had was due in large measure to the talents of its long-running general manager, John O. Grettenberger. Thanks to him, customer satisfaction became an obsession at Cadillac. In the contemporary luxury car market, as Grettenberger himself noted to this writer in an interview, "absolute top quality is really just the price of entry now."

Some of that was in evidence in changes to the product line available in 1994 in addition to the new DeVille.

The base Eldorado and Seville models were upgraded with the Northstar V8, Road Sensing Suspension, and traction control. Remote keyless entry and

1993 Cadillac presidential limousine.

1993 Sedan DeVille special edition.

automatic door locks were made standard. A detuned version of the Corvette 5.7-liter engine made its way under the Fleetwood's gargantuan hood and performance was much improved as a result. A new transmission likewise came with the new engine. Also, the Brougham package included a padded vinyl roof and alloy wheels.

There were very few changes for 1995. Traction control was made standard on the DeVille, Northstar V8 power was increased on the Eldorado and Seville, while electronic chassis controls now evaluated steering angle when deciding what to do with the road sensing suspension, traction control, and ABS. Platinum-tipped spark plugs were added to the Fleetwood, allowing tune-ups to occur every 100,000 miles, and remote keyless entry, central unlocking, and fold-away outside mirrors were added.

For 1996, the Northstar V8 was installed in base DeVille, along with a new transmission, integrated chassis control system, and road-sensing suspension. Meanwhile, the Concours got 25 horsepower boost to 300, along with a higher final-drive ratio for quicker pickup.

The Eldorado and Seville received new seats and seat trim, redesigned sound systems, an (optional) integrated voice-activated cellular phone, daytime running lights, programmable door lock functions and seating positions. The Eldorado Touring Coupe interior was revised, with a center-stack console, bigger gauges, and seamless passenger airbag. The Seville STS also received an updated instrument panel with big gauges and a new center console, the Cadillac-exclusive Rainsense Wiper System (which detects rainfall and turns the wipers on automatically) and a newly improved continuously-variable, road-sensing suspension.

The Fleetwood was in its final year. It was selling well, but the corporation needed the Arlington, Texas, plant in which it was assembled for light truck production. Updates were limited to a new audio system, revised center storage armrest, and pre-wiring for Cadillac's Dual Mode cellular phone.

The DeVille underwent a substantial revamp for 1997, including revised styling, the addition of standard side-impact airbags, and a fresh interior that unfortunately included some of the worst lumbar support seats ever installed in an automobile. A fancier D'elegance model picked up the torch for the late, lamented where the Fleetwood left off. Finally, this was the year that GM really began to make headway with its OnStar services.

There were few important changes in the Eldorado, although it also received the ill-starred lumbar support seats, as did the Seville. In addition, all Sevilles received body structure, suspension, brake system, and interior enhancements. STS models got a new stability enhancement feature designed to correct lateral skids, and road texture detection, which helped modulate the ABS more effectively on rough roads. Programmable memory systems were also new to both models.

The big news, though, was an entirely new product line: the entry-level Catera. It was actually built by GM's Opel affiliate in Germany, although it was designed as a cooperative program between Cadillac and Opel. Opel design and engineering had been very good in those years and the Catera reflected that. The Cadillac contribution was more questionable in certain respects.

The Catera was based on the Opel Omega platform and was built at the

1994 DeVille Concours.

1994 DeVille.

giant Opel plant at Russelsheim, Germany. The chassis, while not innovative, was fully up to snuff for a German sport sedan in that class. Traction control and anti-lock brakes were standard, and particular emphasis was placed on engineering a solid body structure. It showed, for the Catera's body was as tight as anyone could want and as quiet as the proverbial tomb.

Power came from a 3.0-liter, dual-overhead-cam V6 developing 200 horsepower at 6000 rpm. This was not an enormous amount of horsepower and, at 3,770 pounds, the Catera was hardly a lightweight. Still, the engine delivered a wonderfully smooth power flow in all speed ranges—notably including the lower end where so many competitive cars were lacking—with the result that an impressive 0–60 mph time of 8.5 seconds was possible.

Styling is a matter of personal taste. Many observers in the industry had mixed feelings about the Catera in this regard, considering it a shade stubby and bland in appearance, but the reaction it engendered in the general public—passers-by, and so on—was uniformly favorable. No one thought it looked like a Cadillac, but that seemed not to be a major concern. They just liked it.

Still, there were more than a few who regarded the Catera as a bad idea for Cadillac. Their thinking was that the division's most pressing problem was the loss of prestige it suffered in the 1980s (in part due to the Cimarron catastrophe), and that the way to deal with this was to move the brand up in the price spectrum. What Cadillac really needed, if you bought this argument, was an equivalent to the Mercedes-Benz S-Class or the BMW 7-Series. The ill-fated Allanté, which was launched in 1987, failed for a number of reasons, but the biggest one was that Cadillac's prestige had fallen so low that people simply would not pay $55,000 for a Cadillac. Ten years later, they still would not, although the top-end Sevilles were inching in on that territory.

The Catera represented a move in the other direction, being at best irrelevant to Cadillac's most urgent marketing requirement, which was to find a way to compete in the ultra-luxury segment that Mercedes was allowed to develop almost unchallenged in the 1980s. Cadillac officials would have retorted that there were far more sales to be had in the entry-level end of the luxury market—and they would have been right—but the sales potential of a Catera-type vehicle was highly dependent upon the prestige of the nameplate. Most people don't buy a C-Class Mercedes because it is a wonderful car; they buy it because it is the most affordable way to join the elite ranks of Mercedes owners until they can afford a "real" Mercedes, i.e., an E- or an S-Class. Thus, the main sales incentive for the C-Class is the huge prestige of the Mercedes nameplate.

Moreover, with a sticker price of just over $37,000, the Catera was hardly

Top, 1995 Eldorado Touring Coupe; *bottom*, 1995 Sedan DeVille.

inexpensive. In fact, it came in at about two thousand more than a comparably equipped Buick Park Avenue Ultra.

An era came to an end in February, 1997, with the retirement of John Grettenberger. His replacement was John F. Smith, president of Allison Transmission since January, 1994, and General Motors Europe vice president of planning since August, 1989. A native of Kansas City, Missouri, Smith joined General Motors in June 1968 at the former Kansas City Chevrolet assembly plant. He was an engineering student at General Motors Institute (now Kettering University), graduating in 1973. Smith earned a master's degree in business from the Harvard Business School in 1976 and joined the New York Treasurer's Office.

The big news in December, 1997—and for the 1998 model year—was the all-new 1998 Cadillac Seville which went on sale in Japan. This marked the first Cadillac in history to go on sale initially outside the United States. Although Cadillac began producing automobiles in 1903 and exporting them shortly thereafter (they had a London agent at the time they won the first Dewar Trophy in 1908), Cadillac was only now setting its sights on the global arena. From the very beginning of the 1998 Seville program, Cadillac had

1996 Cadillacs equipped with the Northstar engine.

1997 Catera.

committed to a car that would meet the needs and wants of customers in
more than forty countries throughout the world.

In order to emphasize the car's global focus, the world premiere of the 1998
Seville was held in September, 1997, at the Frankfurt International Auto
Show. It was to be offered in three versions for the global market—a North
American model, an international export model and a Japanese model. The
Japanese and international editions were offered in both left- and right-hand
drive. With the addition of right-hand drive models, Seville's presence was designed to increase in many markets including England, South Africa, Malay-
sia, Hong Kong and Singapore. Indeed, the Seville would be Cadillac's first
volume right-hand-drive model since 1941.

1997 Catera interior.

In addition, the international design of the Seville and the growth in overseas markets provided new or expanded opportunities in many left-hand drive markets including South Korea and China. All Sevilles were to be assembled at General Motors' Detroit-Hamtramck Assembly Center and manufactured in full compliance with all applicable legal and market requirements.

The 1998 Seville was positioned as a highly stylized ultimate performance sedan, intended to appeal to non-conservative, independent-thinking individuals looking for a contrast to Mercedes, BMW, Jaguar or Lexus. In the United States, Seville was designed to compete in the sporty luxury segment. Major targeted competitors were the Mercedes-Benz E420, BMW 540i, Lexus LS400, Infiniti Q45, Jaguar XJ and Acura RL.

In Europe, the Seville was intended to compete in the upper two segments, "large" and "exclusive." In Japan, it would compete directly with the Toyota Celsior (Lexus LS400) and Nissan Cima (Infiniti Q45) at the top of Japan's luxury market.

As part of the Seville's move into the global marketplace, distribution became a priority. In the past, Cadillac marketed vehicles outside North America through various independent distributors and franchised retailers. With the introduction of the new Seville, Cadillac was determined to enhance its network of franchised retailers, phasing out a few small independent distributors, and adding retailers in many new regions. Sales outside of North America were expected to increase to one-fifth of Seville's total sales volume over the next several years.

In Europe, the Seville was to be sold through Adam Opel AG and Vauxhall franchised dealerships. The few Cadillac-only franchised dealerships located throughout Europe would continue to sell Cadillacs. In Japan, Seville would continue to be marketed by Yanase, which began selling Cadillacs in 1915. Cadillac regularly exported both right- and left-hand drive cars from 1915 through 1941 to Europe, South America, and various Middle Eastern countries.

To determine the Seville's product direction, research was conducted in several countries, including North American, European and Asian markets. More than four thousand customers participated in fourteen separate clinics. During early research, large-format color slides of 3/8-scale models of various proposals were taken around the world and projected to full size using special equipment. These offered a realistic view of how the finished car might look, allowing potential customers to provide valuable feedback to designers and engineers. Particular attention was paid to owners and lessees of current Sevilles, as well as those of key import competitors.

In addition to the left- and right-hand drive offerings and a reduction in length, other market-specific needs were comprehended in Seville to market it successfully around the world. These included: leaded and unleaded fuel powertrains, integrated rear fog lamps, a radio data system for Europe, a MiniDisc option, power folding outside rear-view mirrors, larger side-view mirrors, a high-speed wiper system, a navigation system for Japan, five language displays (English, French, German, Japanese and Spanish), and several international symbols.

Not surprisingly, the changes in the rest of the Cadillac line were less cosmic. For 1998, StabiliTrak, an integrated chassis control system that corrects four-wheel lateral skids, was made available on the DeVille. New radio systems debuted, and door lock programmability was enhanced, and an idiot light was added to warn about loose fuel caps. Heated seats were added to the d'Elegance and Concours while the Concours also got an alloy wheel redesign. Second-generation airbags also debuted as standard equipment.

In order to satisfy Cadillac customers who were still grumbling about the discontinuance of the rear-Drive Fleetwood and its added size, Cadillac announced what it billed as the largest luxury sedan manufactured in North America: the 1998 Fleetwood Limited. Based on the DeVille platform, the Fleetwood Limited was converted by Superior Coaches of Lima, Ohio, and sold through authorized Cadillac dealers.

Essentially a six-inch stretch edition of the DeVille, the Fleetwood Limited sat on a unique 119.8-inch wheelbase, six inches longer than the standard one. The trunk was also lengthened by six inches, so the overall length of the Fleetwood Limited was a foot more than that of the standard DeVille. As a result, rear-seat leg room was increased by half-a-foot to 49.3 inches, while trunk capacity rose to 23.5 cubic feet.

In addition to stretching the existing Cadillac platform, the Fleetwood Limited featured from a number of strengthened components: heavy-duty suspension and steering systems, special heavy-duty ABS, and heavy-duty cast aluminum wheels of a unique design.

A total production run of 340 was planned for the 1998 model year. Production for 1999 was anticipated at about 800 units. The 1998 Fleetwood Limited carried a base price of $49,995.

There was little new on the Eldorado: A revised interior electrochromic mirror, second-generation airbags and the addition of StabiliTrak to the base model's option list were about it. On the other hand, the "Eldo" was now a unique product by default and no longer shared any sheet metal with any other Cadillac line.

The Catera offered new radios, and a new option was a power rear sunshade. Second-generation airbags had arrived during the middle of the model year.

General Motors, which was turning reorganization into a lifestyle by this point, announced plans to once again restructure its North American Operations Vehicle Sales, Service and Marketing Group. This time the move was away from the traditional nameplate divisions and towards a more highly-integrated field management organization.

The new organization replaced the current five marketing divisions with a

1998 DeVille.

1998 DeVille Concours.

single sales, service and parts field force divided into five regions in the United States. Saturn was to remain an autonomous subsidiary and was not included in the plans.

Said Ronald L. Zarrella, GM vice-president and group executive of North American Vehicle Sales, Service and Marketing:

> The new organization will eliminate hierarchy and reduce structural costs by eliminating overlapping processes and systems and leveraging the talent within this company, giving the dealers an opportunity to maximize their General Motors business. With these changes, we will make better use of technology, eliminate redundancies, and coordinate marketing strategies among brands to move products more efficiently into the marketplace.[2]

Target date for the completed realignment was January 1999. Moreover, the plan called for divisional general managers to be downgraded and no longer have corporate officer status. John F. Smith, general manager of Cadillac Motor Car Division, dodged that bullet. Alone among existing divisional general managers, he retained his status as a vice-president of GM.

This was the last year for the current DeVille, so there were few changes of note. The side airbag deployment now communicated with the optional On-Star communications system, so the outside world would know instantly when you had taken a broadside hit. Comforting, indeed. In the spring, there was a limited run of about 2000 specially-badged-and-optioned Golden Anniversary Edition DeVilles—painted White Diamond with gold trim—to celebrate the nameplate's 50th Anniversary.

The Eldorado's changes were limited to new exterior and interior colors, and a few electronic options.

1998 Seville SLS.

The Seville, which had been entirely new the year before, saw only minor changes. The optional OnStar mobile communications system would automatically notify the OnStar customer assistance center in the case of any airbag deployment, front or side, so that the center could dispatch emergency services to the scene. Previously, notification occurred only with a front airbag deployment. There were also three new exterior colors.

The Catera's "black chrome" grille was darkened this year, while new electronics and emissions systems made the 1999 Catera the first Cadillac to meet the federal Low Emissions Vehicle (LEV) standards. In a move to capture a greater share of the entry-luxury segment, Cadillac added a sport edition and revised marketing efforts in the spring. The Catera Sport went on sale in mid-May, with the extra equipment estimated to add less than $800 to Catera's $34,180 base price. The new model was designed to appeal to the sport-oriented set—thirty-something men and women who enjoyed driving and desired more control behind the steering wheel.

Available in Ebony, Ivory or Platinum exterior paint, the Catera Sport featured 16-inch, 7-spoke aluminum wheels mated to H-rated Goodyear P225/55R16 tires; firmer suspension tuning with automatic load-leveling; specific grille; rear decklid spoiler and more aggressively styled rocker moldings. Interior appointments included black articulating sport leather seats with adjustable thigh bolsters, driver and passenger side-impact airbags (Catera's first) and gun-metal trim.

Cadillac's world was about to change dramatically, though, and it had nothing to do with passenger cars. For several years, the sport-utility boom had been gathering steam and, by the end of the decade, half the vehicles sold in America would be light trucks or SUVs. The luxury segment exploded into life with the 1996 Mercedes-Benz M-Class, growing from just 35,258 units in calendar year 1996 to 92,032 in 1997 as other players entered the fray. This growth was fueled by baby boomers who were moving up from smaller sport-utilities and conventional luxury cars.

Cadillac had not given much thought to this trend. Unfortunately, arch ri-

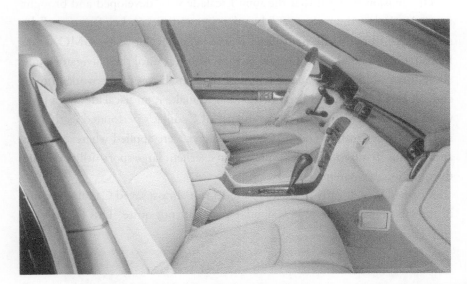

Top, 1998 Seville STS interior; *bottom,* 1998 Seville STS.

val Lincoln had, and so had Cadillac's rivals from Europe and Japan. The Lincoln Navigator burst on the scene as a 1998 model. Based on Ford's hot-selling Expedition full-size SUV, it was an immediate success in the luxury market. Mercedes, which had pioneered the segment in 1996, was soon joined by similar models from Lexus, Infiniti, BMW and others. And suddenly Cadillac's dwindling—but still solid—lead in luxury passenger cars was not enough to keep the marque in the lead in the luxury market sales race.

The division bragged that the 1999 Escalade was "developed and brought to market in less than one year," but that ignored certain key features of the new sport-utility. In the first place, it had been developed by GMC as the Denali. Cadillac had not expressed any interest in it until the Navigator came along, then suddenly a Caddy version of the Denali was in the works. In the end, all that was changed from the Denali to make it an Escalade was a little wood trim in the passenger cabin, the use of Cadillac's perforated leather on seating surfaces and, of course, Cadillac badges were applied wherever it was appropriate. Truth to tell, the result was an excellent large sport-utility despite the questionable parentage.

A rushed launch early in the 1999 model run almost saved Cadillac's bacon in the sales race for the 1998 Calendar year. But not quite. This led to a re-

1999 Eldorado.

markable scandal that would have been unheard-of in previous decades. It was the sort of story that would have brought tears to the eyes of a Chicago ward heeler. Your party's about to lose? Not to worry! Stuff the ballot box! What is a few thousand votes in a good cause, anyway?

This appears to have been more or less what happened in the final weeks of 1998 when those responsible for compiling General Motors sales figures for the press realized Cadillac was about to lose its long-held position as America's leader in luxury vehicle sales to arch-rival Lincoln. In an internal audit, GM officials discovered that the previously reported number of deliveries of Cadillac vehicles by Cadillac dealers to their customers in December, 1998, were "overstated due to an improper reporting process." That is the nicer way to put it.

Explained Roy S. Roberts, vice-president and group executive, GM North American Vehicle Sales, Service and Marketing:

> We regret that the inflated delivery report caused the media, in particular, to believe that Cadillac dealers had indeed sold more vehicles in December, and thus for the entire 1998 calendar year, than Lincoln. Winning in the marketplace obviously is very important to us, but nothing is more important than our integrity, whether it's the product we put on the road or how we represent ourselves in the reporting of our results. General Motors will assure the process for reporting dealer sales will be accurate.[3]

Roberts added that John F. Smith, general manager of Cadillac, had notified Mark Hutchins, the president of Ford's Lincoln Mercury Division, of the findings and had apologized by letter.

What GM's errant statisticians did was take 4,773 Cadillac sales from January and record them as December sales. Two things resulted: 1) Cadillac claimed a squeaker of a victory (by a margin of 222 units) over Lincoln in January–December sales, and 2) Cadillac's reported sales for the First Quarter of 1999 looked dreadful.

Indeed, Cadillac, with 182,570 cars sold in 1998 easily beat out Lincoln's 143,262 cars. The overall Lincoln total—186,191 vehicles—included tens of thousands of units of its popular Navigator sport utility, which, by any standard, were trucks. So, in the end Cadillac sold the most luxury cars and Lincoln sold the most luxury vehicles of all types. Cadillac had been the leader in luxury cars sales in America for sixty-three years, ever since it introduced the highly-successful Series 60 in 1936.

For 2000, the DeVille was all-new inside and out and showcased new automotive technologies such as Night Vision, Ultrasonic Rear Parking Assist and the newest generation of GM's StabiliTrak traction-control system. It also boasted improvements to the Northstar V8 that not only improved fuel economy, but made this engine operate even smoother than before.

The 2000 DeVille was available in three models: DeVille, DeVille DHS (High Luxury Sedan) and DeVille DTS (Touring Sedan). The DTS was specifically aimed at baby boomers moving up. In other words, Cadillac was attempting to sell traditional American luxury car virtues of comfort and convenience to a crowd that has high expectations for ride, handling and performance. Needless to say, this was also a group that tended to think of Cadillac—when they thought of it at all—with contempt. Yet, this is the group that would fuel most luxury car sales in coming years as the older, current crop of luxury car buyers died off. If Cadillac was to have a future, GM desperately needed to find a way to connect with these people. Hence, the DTS.

Another way of doing that was by positioning Cadillac as an engineering/technology leader. The division described its new DeVille as "a showcase for pioneering intuitive technology that brings meaningful benefits to customers." (Was this a slap at Mercedes and the obsession on the part of the folks in Stuttgart with techno-overkill?) Two of the key features in this techno showcase were electronic options: Night Vision and Ultrasonic Rear Parking Assist. A standard feature was OnStar, GM's information and communications service.

1999 Escalade.

Additional technology built into the new DeVille included safety-cage construction, leading-edge passive restraints, a CD-based navigation system and OnStar. The DeVille also featured the auto industry's first light emitting diode (LED) taillight and center high-mounted stoplight combination, which the division claimed was a safety benefit because of a quicker "on time" compared to incandescent bulbs.

The 2000 DeVille benefited from a new body architecture that was notably stiffer in both torsion and handling. Noise, vibration and harshness control were superb. The quietness of the DeVille's ride was in marked contrast to recent Cadillac models, even very good ones like the Seville STS, that were still much noisier than their competitors. No more. Once again, we saw evidence of real progress at GM.

Cadillac's much-touted 4.6-liter, 300 horsepower Northstar V8 was redesigned for better mileage with regular fuel, smoother and quieter operation, and the DeVille was now certified as a low emissions vehicle (LEV) for California and Northeast states. A highway economy figure of 28 miles-per-gallon (mpg) in such a car would have been considered astonishing a few years ago. The contemporary Mercedes CL500 coupe, for example, had an essentially similar 5.0-liter V8 rated at 302 horsepower and claimed 23 mpg on the open road.

The 2000 DeVille also featured StabiliTrak 2.0, the latest evolution of Cadillac's active-suspension stability-control system. It was enhanced for 2000 with the addition of active steering effort compensation, which slightly increased turning effort during sudden maneuvers, and side-slip-rate control, which responded to traction loss at all four wheels by gently applying both front brakes to help the driver regain control. In addition, the DTS featured the second generation of Cadillac's continuously variable road sensing suspension, CVRSS 2.0.

Inside, the 2000 DeVille offered all the sybaritic luxury one would expect. Features included three-zone climate control, adaptive seating, massaging lumbar seats and a new flexible center seat and storage system. The rear seat incorporated theater seating layout for optimum visibility, heated seats and power lumbar adjustments.

For several years, GM had been reducing the number of platforms for all brands. Cadillac had been using at least three for its bread-and-butter sedans. With the 2000 range, the division was reduced to one, with the old rear-drive Fleetwood but a memory and the DeVille now using the same platform as the Seville. As a result, the new DeVille was more than two inches shorter and narrower than the car it replaced. On the other hand, its wheelbase was actually 1.5 inches longer, and there was virtually the same amount of interior space as before.

As for the styling, it exhibited a high degree of crowd appeal, even if it was a bit of a "college design"—as one former GM designer put it—i.e., as something a design student might have done but hardly the work of a master. At best, the DeVille's design had a sort of big car heft to it without achieving either beauty or elegance.

As for the Eldorado, GM had a change of heart. Early in the 1999 model

Top, 2000 DeVille DTS interior; *bottom*, 2000 DeVille DTS.

run, the division told its dealers not to expect a 2000 model. In the spring the word is that there would be one and, moreover, that a production run of 17,000 units was projected. Eventually, production was shifted out of the Hamtramck plant in Detroit to GM's Lansing Craft Centre where the company added approximately 250 jobs to handle the work. GM invested approximately $28 million to make the move, and the Eldorado lasted until the end of the 2002 model run.

For 2000, the Northstar V8s were improved, and the standard Eldorado received a new logo: ESC (for Eldorado Sport Coupe). The racy Eldorado Touring Coupe (ETC) landed exterior enhancements, such as body-color fascia moldings and side inserts (replacing chrome), new seven-spoke wheels with Cadillac logos in the center caps, and a new ETC decklid logo.

The Northstar V8s were also improved on the Seville line, and all models got a new airbag suppression system and the revised version of GM's Stabili-Trak. A new ultrasonic rear parking assist feature and an advanced navigation system were optional on both STS and SLS. There were also two new exterior colors.

Mildly successful front and rear styling enhancements and a revised interior updated the Catera for 2000. Side airbags were standard on all models, and an optional sport package finally arrived with 17-inch wheels, heated sport seats, a spoiler, rocker panel extensions, xenon HID headlights and

2001 Cadillac presidential limousine.

brushed-aluminum interior trim. Electronic drive-by-wire throttle control and a revised torque converter improved "oomph" off the line. Revised suspension tuning better controlled ride motions and body roll, while tightened steering improved road feel.

The big change for the 2000 Escalade was the availability of vertical-split rear cargo doors in addition to the standard split-tailgate rear-hatch design. The changes for the following model year were just about as minor.

In February, 2000, General Manager John Smith moved on in the GM system and was replaced by Michael O'Malley. O'Malley was not named a vice-president of the corporation thus ending a status Cadillac general managers had enjoyed for decades.

After a complete redesign for 2000, changes on the DeVille line consisted of: a tire pressure monitoring system as an available option, Graphite replaced Parisian Blue and Polo Green paint schemes, Dark Gray was added as an interior color and all Devilles were now certified throughout the U.S. as low-emissions vehicles (LEV).

Only three minor changes appeared on the Eldorado: Sequoia was added for an exterior color, Dark Gray was added for the interior and the Bose sound system with mini-disc player went away.

Tire pressure monitoring was now available on the Seville STS, as well as an e-mail-capable Infotainment radio, a hands-free integrated cellular phone, 17-inch chrome wheels and high-intensity discharge headlamps. OnStar in-vehicle safety, security and information service were now standard fare on the STS and available on the SLS. Two new SLS and three STS packages rounded out the changes.

After mildly successful front and rear styling enhancements and a revised interior for 2000, the 2001 model year brought few changes for the Catera. OnStar 2.6 in-vehicle safety, security and information service, vented rear disc brakes and the Solar Protect windshield were now standard on all models. The Catera Sport model received new seats and projector beam headlamps were now standard on the base Catera.

The final grace note of the closing century—or the opening one of the next—was the debut of a Cadillac "New Millennium" Presidential Limousine. A spanking new Cadillac limousine carried President George W. Bush during his inaugural parade. This vehicle was the first Cadillac to carry the division's new wreath and crest emblem, and was the latest in a long series of presidential Cadillacs.

The new limousine had the exterior appearance of the production 2001 DeVille with handcrafted construction under the skin. This limousine was considerably longer, wider and taller than the production models. Its interior boasted seven-passenger seating with improved comfort and visibility for all occupants. Many of the interior cues, including the instrument panel and trim, were the same or similar to the production DeVille. Wood accents and blue leather and cloth complete the interior. A rear seat executive package featured a concealed, foldaway desktop that could be deployed when needed. The rear seats had an adjustable reclining feature and the Cadillac adaptive seat system for added comfort.

An embroidered presidential seal was positioned in the center of the rear seat back panel, as well as on each rear door trim panel. Presidential seals were also affixed to the exterior rear doors. The U.S. flag was placed on the right front fender, and the presidential standard was located on the left front fender. Flush-mounted spotlights in the fenders illuminated the flags at night.

Cadillac General Manager Michael J. O'Malley said:

> Just as Air Force One is a flying Oval Office, this new Cadillac provides the same amenities for our nation's leader while traveling on the ground.[4]

CHAPTER ELEVEN

Bob Lutz with the Cadillac Sixteen concept car.

Looking to the Future:
2002–Up

ENTERING THE NEW MILLENNIUM, Cadillac was in the middle of the most brutal fight for luxury market leadership it had ever known. Those who plotted the marque's fortunes staked everything on a new concept they called "art and science." Throughout its history, they reasoned, beautiful and classic Cadillac designs coupled with numerous advanced technology breakthroughs had been the hallmarks of the brand's rich history. And this pedigree of creating true "art and science" in its products would serve as the focal point for a new brand direction that would elevate Cadillac's global stature as the world's premier luxury vehicle manufacturer.

John F. Smith, Cadillac's general manager when the concept was developed, had explained it this way:

> While it's a very simple and concise statement, "art and science" is really about focusing the division's internal and external efforts to deliver a product and ownership experience that will be unmatched.
>
> We're looking to our past for the spirit of inspiration and creativity to rekindle the Cadillac mystique. But this is not a "retro" statement; this is completely forward focused. For the thousands of people who design, engineer and make Cadillacs every day, "art and science" is meant to be a

touchstone. We want them all to keep the concept in mind whenever they think of Cadillac.[1]

The "art and science" positioning also will be expressed in communications about the brand to distinguish Cadillac from other luxury automakers. Smith continued:

"Art" is that visual distinction, that flair, that attitude, that sets Cadillac apart from competitors who are likely to be given to understatement, because of the conservative tastes of their home-market customers.

   "'Science' builds on the global credibility of America's pre-eminence in the sciences, annually showcased in the Nobel Prize awards. Combined, "art and science" is a uniquely American proposition, as evidenced by accomplishments in architecture, space exploration, aircraft design, software and movies.[2]

As a core part of Cadillac's brand essence, "art and science" is intended to build on Cadillac's history and form the basis to grow globally and to leverage new-found strength and leadership at home. Smith added:

For many customers, Cadillac is associated with striking, glamorous, beautiful vehicles. Many people also remember seeing equipment and technology on Cadillacs that had never been seen anywhere else. For example, while the Harley Earl-inspired 1959 Eldorado featured the unforgettable tail-fin art form, it also introduced new technology like intermittent windshield wipers and six-way power seats; science solutions that, today, we take for granted in vehicles across the full price spectrum.[3]

Among Cadillac's many other innovations, it was the first automaker to use a self-starter, the first with an independent front-wheel suspension and first with the Syncro-Mesh transmission. Cadillac offered the first mass-produced V8 engine and the first mass-produced vehicle stability system. Translating traditional Cadillac flair into contemporary terms is the challenge for designers. Added Smith:

The specifics change over time, as to what constitutes art in one time frame, or for one generation versus another. But the notion of "flair" gives us an advantage. It's certainly something we need to do as it relates to our own home market, because it would not make sense to emulate the import luxury brands. If we cease to be ourselves, we take away the reason for somebody to consider us.[4]

Smith noted that consumers around the world recognized America's expertise in science in areas such as computer software and the defense industry. The challenge facing Cadillac's designers and engineers was to translate that into future Cadillac products. Smith concluded:

We think we can distinguish ourselves by bringing to our cars the very best America has to offer in the sciences, science being the foundation for anything done with engineering or technology.

Managing that task was now the responsibility of Mark R. LaNeve who was appointed general manager of Cadillac on May 1, 2001. A native of Pennsylvania, LaNeve held several sales and marketing positions at Cadillac between 1981 and 1995. He then left GM to accept an appointment as vice president of marketing at Volvo Cars of North America, Inc. (VCNA). He subsequently rose to president and CEO. He left Volvo to accept the top slot at Cadillac.

Many steps had been taken to put the marque firmly on the course that was to define its future, some portentous, some silly. Among the latter was the decision to revise the famed Cadillac crest. It seems that whenever companies are in trouble they change their logos—as if the logo attached to the product is the problem rather than the other way around. The best that can be said for Cadillac's attempt is that little damage was done.

The Cadillac emblem has been modified approximately thirty times during the company's history in order to reflect the evolution of the brand and vehicle design, the tastes of the times, and the inability of Cadillac executives to leave well enough alone. The previous version had been adopted in 1963.

The redesigned logo was streamlined and simplified to incorporate bold, crisp angles that, Cadillac said, reflect its future design philosophy. Noted then General Manager John F. Smith:

> The new wreath and crest depicts a forward-looking and youthful image while maintaining distinctiveness and a sense of prestige. It reflects Cadillac's new design direction and underscores our technological reach—key elements of our vision to be a leader in the global luxury market through the application of art and science.[5]

The Cadillac script, which in the past accompanied the wreath and crest, was not changed. Cadillac vehicles began donning the new wreath and crest in the 2002 model year, coinciding with the celebration of Cadillac's centennial. The division planned to incorporate the art and science look and feel into its dealership facilities during the same time frame.

The original Cadillac crest, which was trademarked in 1906 was derived from the coat of arms of Le Sieur Antoine de la Mothe Cadillac, who founded the city of Detroit in 1701 and for whom the brand is named. Despite repeated tampering over the years, it has changed remarkably little. The modified design eliminates the couronne, or Coronet, and the birds, called "merlettes," that appeared in the first and fourth quarterings.

The new crest retains the old color scheme—black against gold—which denotes wisdom and riches; red, indicating prowess and boldness in action; silver, indicating purity, charity, virtue and plenty; and blue, indicating knightly valor. The background of the wreath and crest is platinum.

The first look at what the art and science approach would mean for future products was revealed at the 1999 auto shows in the nature of the Cadillac Evoq, a luxury roadster concept.

Evoq (pronounced "evoke") also showcased a next generation of the respected Cadillac Northstar V8 engine in a rear-wheel drive configuration. It was the first true Cadillac concept car in more than ten years. Said Smith:

> In a pure design sense, this concept evokes Cadillac's significant heritage of design leadership without at all being "retro." In creating Evoq, we're interpreting in a very modern way the attitude and flair of great Cadillacs from the past. Its evocative design is a clear forerunner of future Cadillacs as we develop our global luxury brand strategy.[6]

Kip Wasenko, Evoq's chief designer, said the challenge was to capture the emotion of great Cadillac designs from the past in an entirely modern expression. The visual brand character cues include elements such as vertical head lamps and tail lamps, a tapering sail, a strong spline emphasis on the body, and the distinctive Cadillac badge and grille. Wasenko said:

2002 Eldorado Touring Coupe.

We're exploring a style that draws heavily on design cues from the past, but interpreted in a completely forward-looking, hi-tech package. That's the magic of Evoq—it's a bold direction for Cadillac design that is very fresh and compelling. The effect is very crisp, very tailored and simply unique. Look closely and use your imagination as to future product directions. These design cues will take Cadillac into the next century.[7]

The Evoq was followed two years later with another concept, the Imaj—as in "image" the way the French say it. Introduced at Geneva, the Imaj concept vehicle was yet the latest salvo in Cadillac's effort to redefine itself and the way people think of the division.

The Imaj was a descendant of the recent Evoq concept car, but—according to Cadillac's overworked PR types—was said to have its spiritual roots in the era of Harley Earl. In contrast to the Evoq, the Imaj was more of a limousine than a high-tech roadster. Its design was meant to permit it to be chauffeur-driven during the week, while its owner toiled away on the Internet in the back seat. And, in the words of Cadillac's logorrheic press release, "when it's time to leave work behind, you can leave the chauffeur behind as well, and escape into the mountains or down a coastal highway." Perhaps more easily said than done if you're carrying an entire office in the passenger compartment, but an interesting notion.

2002 Escalade.

The Imaj featured interior appointments of brushed aluminum, wood and Scottish Bridge of Weir leather. An electrochromatic roof could be adjusted to allow sunlight or privacy, while each passenger rated his own individually adjustable set of roof louvers. A Bose audio system using no fewer than seventeen speakers, along with some brand-new signal processing hardware, provided the sound. And, perhaps best of all, there was a custom-made set of Bvlgari luggage, designed to mimic the outer form of the car. The Italian jewelry designer also provided the car's instrument design and clock.

Getting back to the real world, a few months later GM announced plans to produce a low-volume, two-seat Cadillac luxury roadster for the 2003 model year on a dedicated assembly line at the Corvette assembly plant in Bowling Green, Kentucky. The rear-wheel-drive roadster is inspired by the Evoq concept car, press reaction to the Imaj having been less than idolatrous.

It was announced that this new Cadillac flagship would be developed on the next generation of GM's performance car architecture, which was specifically designed for convertible applications. The vehicle architecture would feature advanced steel hydroforming, an aluminum cockpit structure and cored composite floors, making it exceptionally stiff, crashworthy and lightweight.

While strongly influenced by the Evoq concept, the drop top picked up many technology and styling enhancements not featured in the concept. Chief among these was a one-button fully automatic folding hard-top. The interior

2002 Escalade EXT.

2003 CTS.

would also feature instrumentation fashioned by Bvlgari, the renowned Italian jeweler. In addition, the car would feature several exclusive Cadillac technologies, including the 4.6-liter Northstar V8 in its first production rear-wheel-drive configuration, mated to an electronic five-speed automatic transmission with manual mode in a trans-axle configuration.

Other elements of the Northstar System, such as MagneRide active suspension damping and the StabiliTrak yaw control system would be standard on the vehicle as well as Michelin's revolutionary run-flat PAX tire system. Night Vision would also be available. The price was expected to be competitive with the Mercedes SL 500, the Jaguar XK8 and the Lexus SC 430.

The vehicle line executive (VLE) for the Cadillac luxury roadster was David Hill, who would head the vehicle development team. As the lead engineer on the latest generation of the Corvette, Hill brought extensive vehicle development experience, including twenty-seven years with Cadillac. Chief engineer was David Leone, another Cadillac veteran. Tom Peters, one of the most passionate and versatile talents in GM Design, was responsible for the interior and exterior design development. Marketing veteran Jay Spenchian would be the luxury roadster's brand manager. Spenchian also had responsibility for Cadillac's much-anticipated entry luxury sedan—the CTS.

Before the CTS could happen, though, a new factory had to be built on a site chosen in Lansing, Michigan. The all-new assembly plant, according to the company, would be designed to bring together many of the best, most competitive manufacturing practices from around the globe. The Lansing Grand

River (LGR) Assembly Plant (as it would be know) would be GM's first new assembly plant in the United States since the Saturn plant in Spring Hill, Tennessee, built in 1986. It would build the next generation Cadillac Catera and other luxury vehicles.

The plant would consist of three separate buildings—a body shop, paint shop and general assembly—designed around lean manufacturing processes. GM was planning to invest about $558 million in the project, including buildings and equipment. Production was targeted to begin in the fourth quarter of 2001, and the plant was projected to employ 1,500 people by its third year of operation.

In bringing together what it called "global best practices," GM was adopting manufacturing processes developed at its plant in Eisenach, Germany, which was highly regarded for its efficiency. Process improvements from the company's newer plants in Poland, Argentina, China, Brazil and Thailand would be incorporated as well. The company expected to realize broad gains in the areas of "people" systems, quality, customer responsiveness and cost and safety.

The first product to be built in the new plant was destined to be the 2003 Cadillac CTS. The replacement for the Catera, the CTS, made its debut at the Pebble Beach Concours d'Elegance in Monterey, California. Cadillac hailed it the "first 100 percent application" of its art and science approach to passenger car design. Said Mark R. LaNeve, Cadillac's general manager:

> In our first century of existence, many memorable designs have set Cadillac apart from the other luxury cars in the crowd. CTS will turn heads in a segment that typically refines, rather than defines, automotive styling. It's a modern interpretation of the strikingly beautiful cars for which Cadillac became famous. In short, it's a classic Cadillac for the 21st century.[8]

Built on an all-new rear-drive platform, the CTS is available with a manual transmission mated to a 3.2-liter V6 that powers it from 0–60 mph in less than seven seconds. The CTS also represents a sea change in Cadillac nomenclature. Said LaNeve:

> As part of our global initiative, this car will sell alongside other Cadillacs in showrooms in Europe and Asia. Customers in other parts of the world are accustomed to alphanumeric names for their vehicles, and, eventually, all our vehicles will have names that reflect our global nature.[9]

The Cadillac design team gave CTS a look all its own. It reflects the current Cadillac design philosophy first showcased on the Evoq concept car, one that communicates American technology and science. From computer-generated forms to high-tech, aerospace-influenced materials and textiles, these designs are intended to showcase technology and an overt expression of craftsmanship. For CTS, claims Cadillac, the result is a "standout exterior design that features crisp intersections, a short front overhang and sharp edges that produce a dia-mond-like quality, yet in a clean, simple, uncluttered presentation."

The CTS design team had two objectives for the profile view: Use the fea-ture line as the dominant theme, and accentuate the stance of the vehicle. The rear track of CTS is a fixed design point, as is the fender flare. The vehicle sides were tucked in slightly to enhance that flare for a more tailored look. The sail panel also enhances the "fast formal" look, giving CTS a sportier appearance.

Cadillac's traditional vertical headlights and taillights first appeared on Cadillacs in 1965. CTS' integrated headlights convey the high-tech image of op-tical instruments and high-end camera lenses. Thin and tall, they create more space for the large louvered egg-crate grille—another Cadillac staple, this one dating back to 1933. The shield-shaped grille houses the new wreath and crest and has a V-shaped bottom. The rear view complements the front, with a full-color wreath and crest on the center line and a full-width V-shaped CHMSL.

The interior provides all the amenities that luxury customers have come to expect, with the emphasis on comfort and convenience. It makes use of warm, rich, inviting materials and colors, using wood only in areas where the cus-tomer will contact it, such as on the steering wheel, shifter knob and door pulls.

Designed from the ground up with an exclusive rear-wheel-drive architec-ture, the new CTS was tested extensively and refined on Germany's famed Nürburgring. The Sigma platform has been especially designed for rear-wheel drive vehicles, and can accommodate all-wheel drive as well.

The new 3.2-liter V6 powering CTS in North America is a completely re-engineered version of the 3.0-liter V6 in its predecessor. The engine develops 220 hp at 6000 rpm and 218 lb-ft of torque at 3400 rpm. The engine has been fully revised to improve driveability, power, torque and emissions. While most V6 engines use a 60-degree inclination, the CTS team chose a 54-degree bank angle to accommodate the packaging requirements of CTS. The 54-degree an-gle between the cylinder banks is unique among GM four-camshaft V6s. This compact packaging makes it appropriate for both front- and rear-drive.

The engine is mated to either a five-speed manual or five-speed automatic transmission. The five-speed manual from Getrag uses a rod-actuated shift linkage. The five-speed electronically-controlled automatic transmission—the 5L40-E Hydra-Matic—is a first for GM. The same transmission is also used in the BMW 5-Series and X5 SUV. The 5L40-E features a full complement of ad-vanced electronic control capabilities, including a shift mode button that allows the driver to select between "Sport," "Winter" and "Economy" modes, shift patterns that adapt to driving conditions and driver style, traction control capability, engine torque management during shifts, and powertrain protection capabilities. Another electronic feature is also a first for GM: engine braking in all five gears, giving the automatic the same sporty feel as a downshifting manual. The 5L40-E also has the unique ability, in Sport mode, to identify high-performance inputs from the driver and hold a gear indefinitely through a corner after the driver's foot is lifted off the accelerator pedal.

Yet still more is in the pipeline for 2004. Cadillac will get a new crossover utility vehicle—the Cadillac SRX. The SRX will enter the medium luxury utility field, one of the fastest emerging market segments. The SRX will position Cadillac to compete in a segment it is not in today and form a bridge between Cadillac's premium entry- and full-size sedans and its powerful utilities. It will be built on the new Sigma platform at GM's new state-of-the-art Lansing Grand River Facility. Versions with V6 and V8 power will be offered, and it will be available in AWD and RWD configurations, as well.

Perhaps the most exciting possibility in Cadillac's "art and science" future was revealed at the 2003 North American International Auto Show: the Sixteen. Cadillac's modern era began back in 1934 when Nick Dreystadt was named general manager and the Cadillac Sixteen was the top-end model. Could history be repeating itself? Yes, according to Robert A. Lutz, GM's vice-chairman for product development and chairman of GM North America:

2004 SRX.

2004 SLR.

The Sixteen is a modern interpretation of everything that made Cadillac the standard of the world and can again. It's a reminder of a glorious past as well as a progressive statement. Cadillac's tradition is rich, but in the next several years it will be introducing vehicles as solid, dynamic and beautifully designed as anything it's ever done. And Sixteen is a harbinger of this new era.[10]

Sweet V16.

The name speaks to the car's powerful sixteen-cylinder, 1000 horsepower engine and Cadillac's heritage as a maker of fine luxury automobiles. Cadillac's reputation grew exponentially during the 1930s in no small part because of the development of the automotive industry's first V16. The Cadillac Sixteen's grand exterior proportions create an unparalleled presence; its splendid interior is meticulously handcrafted and urbane.

Said Brian Smith, the Cadillac Sixteen's exterior designer:

The Cadillac Sixteen proportions were crafted with great attention to detail and homage to classic design. The Cadillac Sixteen evokes an era when luxury cars were hand-built.[11]

General Motors' designers drew extensively on the traditions of the coach-built era in crafting the Cadillac Sixteen, employing the distinctive talents of leading artisans for the upholstery, instrumentation, interior wood and metal elements, and aluminum body panels.

As an exterior statement, the Cadillac Sixteen's proportional composition is bold. The aluminum hood is long, giving the car tremendous dash-to-axle dimension; the wheel arches were designed to accommodate the beautiful 24-inch polished aluminum wheels. The four-door hardtop incorporates an all-glass roof and is without B-pillars. Crisp-edged lines of the midnight silver aluminum body panels accentuate the Cadillac Sixteen's striking appearance.

Even the engine compartment, with its sculpted design, has drama. With dual panels hinged about a center spine that runs the length of the expansive hood, it makes an event out of opening the engine bay. The hood panels are power-operated.

Said Wayne Cherry, GM's vice president of design:

> The engine bay really pays tribute to the V16. It's like a setting for a diamond, clean and simple. The under-hood was designed with the same care and attention as the interior.
>
> The interior is a pure expression of design. Premium materials in luxury refinement are fine woods, precision-cut metals and crystal. They've all been combined and balanced in harmony in the Cadillac Sixteen.[12]

The interior theme is evocative of the posh accommodations of 1930s era Cadillacs, but with contemporary style. For instance, the dashboard features a center-mounted Bvlgari clock.

Top, Sixteen concept car interior; *bottom*, Sixteen concept car.

The hand-stitched, Tuscany leather upholstered seats nestle the occupants. The right rear seat features power adjustable slope to recline like a chaise lounge. Warm, hand-woven silk carpets the floor in a light cream color that matches the leather upholstery. The dash, door panels, and front and rear consoles are trimmed with walnut burl veneer inlays.

Said Eric Clough, the Sixteen's interior designer:

> The lighting is architectural, enhancing the mood and desirability of the Cadillac Sixteen's interior space, complementing its shapes and colors. Technique combines with technology for a sophisticated, pampered ambiance.[13]
>
> Meanwhile, the custom-designed crystal on the cluster dials offers subtle cues of the Cadillac Sixteen's precise engineering, elegance and craftsmanship.

While GM designers drew inspiration from the ultra-luxury sedan's ancestry, the Cadillac Sixteen is thoroughly modern in its powerplant and technological content.

The Cadillac Sixteen's 32-valve V16 concept engine displaces 13.6 liters and is mated to a four-speed electronically controlled automatic transmission. The engine features fuel-saving Displacement on Demand technology, debuting in 2004 on some 2005 GM models, which shuts down half of the cylinders during most driving conditions and automatically and seamlessly reactivates them for more demanding conditions, such as brisk acceleration or load hauling cylinders when the driver needs the engine's full power. The engine produces 1000 horsepower and 1000 lbs.-ft. of torque.

The extensive use of aluminum components and structure provide substantial weight advantages. The aluminum-steel chassis employs high-arm SLA suspension up front and independent semi-trailing arm suspension in the rear. Four-wheel steering enhances the Cadillac Sixteen's maneuverability. The front and rear brakes are six-piston calipers with 16-inch rotors.

Electronic amenities include a rear-seat DVD information system, Bose sound system, and the fifth-generation OnStar in-vehicle safety and security communication system. The head and tail lamps feature LED technology.

All told, the Cadillac Sixteen is an ultra-luxury automobile of the first order. Concluded Cherry:

> This car offers premier refinement and craftsmanship. Its ultra-contemporary technical detailing is evident throughout. The Cadillac Sixteen is befitting of the great Cadillac tradition as the standard of the world.[14]

It remains to be seen what all these ambitious efforts will lead to. One thing is certain: GM is not about to give up luxury market leadership without a fight.

Notes

CHAPTER ONE, 1946–47

The most important resources drawn upon in the writing of this chapter include the Federal Trade Commission's *Report on Motor Vehicle Industry*, the author's interview with Cadillac designer Frank Hershey, and the author's collection of General Motors- and Cadillac-related material.

1. When Edsel Ford died of cancer in May, 1943, the Ford family reportedly was loathe to have him buried out of a Cadillac hearse. Unfortunately, they discovered, all the local funeral homes had switched over to Cadillac equipment by that point. Accordingly, a frantic search for a Henney-built Packard was launched. In the end, one was found—in Chicago—and had to be rushed overnight to Detroit for the funeral.

2. Canada, as a member of the British Commonwealth, had been officially at war since September, 1939.

3. General Motors Corp. papers, author's collection.

CHAPTER TWO, 1948–49

The most important resources drawn upon in the writing of this chapter include the author's interviews with Semon Knudsen and with designers Frank Hershey and Strother MacMinn, and the author's collection of General Motors- and Cadillac-related material.

1. Hershey interview, author's collection.

2. Ibid.

3. Knudsen interview, author's collection.

4. Perhaps this dynamic can be better understood by using a modern analogy. Lexus and Infiniti are regarded today throughout the industry as direct competitors; they spanned roughly the same price spectrum when they were launched in 1990 and their flagship models (the LS400/SC400 and the Q45, respectively) are positioned in roughly the same price segment at the top. But, since 1990, Infiniti has moved down scale. The G20—priced well below anything Lexus offers, well below even the "near" luxury segment—now accounts for one-third of Infiniti sales. Meanwhile, the Q45 (13,820 units in 1992) has never come close to matching Lexus 400 series in sales

(53,2380 units in 1992). Thus, nearly everyone in the industry continues to regard the two as direct competitors despite the fact that, in the true luxury market, Lexus outsells Infiniti by nearly four-to-one, and despite the fact that fully one-third of Infiniti sales are mid-priced cars sold for thousands less than any Lexus.

5. The Seventy-Fives were given new instrument panels in 1948 and 1949 in order to keep them looking at least somewhat contemporary, at least from inside.

6. A fair number of Coupe de Villes and Rivieras have survived but, curiously, the Holidays—which may have been the best-looking of the group—have almost disappeared.

CHAPTER THREE, 1950–53

The most important resources drawn upon in the writing of this chapter include the author's interviews with Semon Knudsen and Strother MacMinn, and the author's collection of General Motors- and Cadillac-related material.

1. Very heavily reworked. Still, the cowl and instrument panel were basically interchangeable from 1949 to 1950—and that is always a dead give-away, as the cowl is one of the most complex and expensive stampings in a car.

2. General Motors' Harrison division pioneered the engine-mounted system in general use today. It was first used by Pontiac in 1954, then slowly spread to the other divisions. Cadillac got it in 1957.

CHAPTER FOUR, 1954–58

The most important resources drawn upon in the writing of this chapter include the author's interviews with Strother MacMinn, Richard Stout and Charles Jordan, and the author's collection of General Motors- and Cadillac-related material.

1. Curiously, De Soto also used the Seville name in 1956 for its top-end Firedome series hardtops. Apparently, someone dropped the ball at the manufacturers' association that kept track of such things and was supposed to prevent duplications. In 1960, for example, both Ford and Plymouth wanted to use the Falcon name for their compacts, but Ford got it listed first, and so Plymouth had to settle for calling its compact the Valiant. How Cadillac and Chrysler each continued to build Imperials for so many years is open to conjecture (Cadillac's model had been in the catalog since 1917, while Chrysler's first Imperial dated from 1926). In any case, De Soto dropped the Seville designation in 1957 and Cadillac ceased using the Imperial model name in 1959.

2. This show car was later sold and, painted Bat Black, was used as the basis for the Batmobile in the 1960s television series.

CHAPTER FIVE, 1959–64

The most important resources drawn upon in the writing of this chapter include the author's collection of General Motors- and Cadillac-related material.

1. Raymond Loewy received most of the credit, but it was Exner's group that did most of the work.

2. General Motors Corp. papers, author's collection.

3. Jordan interview, author's collection.

4. Jordan interview, author's collection.

5. The total run of the 1958 Chevy/Pontiac A-body would be exactly one model year, the briefest tenure for a unique production body shell in the history of the corporation, before or since.

CHAPTER SIX, 1965–70

The most important resources drawn upon in the writing of this chapter include the author's collection of General Motors- and Cadillac-related material.

1. Ironically, and tragically, one of the factors that contributed to Lincoln's growing public recognition was the assassination of President Kennedy in Dallas in a specially-built Continental, although certainly no one at Ford could have wanted it that way. Henry Ford II had broken with his family's Republican tradition to become a vocal Kennedy supporter in 1960, while Robert McNamara, who had played so important a role in the design of the car itself, had left Ford to become Kennedy's Secretary of Defense.

2. This treatment had been pioneered at General Motors on the highly-regarded 1963 Pontiac full-size cars.

3. Whatever that was. Anyone ever see a Tamo tree?

4. The one-piece interior door panels irritated many Cadillac enthusiasts at the time who took this as a sign, not of progress, but of cheapness.

5. According to David Holls, one-time director of design at General Motors, William Mitchell, previously chief designer of the Cadillac styling studio and then vice-president of design at General Motors, wanted the big Pontiac to re-create the frontal feel of the prewar La Salle, with its high and narrow center grille section. It was, in fact, the first tentative attempt to bring back something akin to the traditional radiator shell look, and would reach full flower on the 1970 full-size Pontiacs. Whatever it may have done for La Salle, the look did little for Pontiac.

6. This writer, having owned examples from every year in the 1967–71 period, would agree.

7. The Cadillac showroom brochure this year, incidentally, is a poor guide to authenticity on these cars; styling mock-ups were used and showed several models with incorrect trim, while the Calais and Coupe de Ville two-door hardtops were four-door hardtops on the side facing away from the camera!

CHAPTER SEVEN, 1971–79

The most important resources drawn upon in the writing of this chapter include the author's interview with William Hoglund, and the author's collection of General Motors- and Cadillac-related material.

1. The La Salle name was seriously considered for the Seville. It was dropped when market research revealed that, to the buying public, it meant "cheap Cadillac."

2. Jordan interview, author's collection.

3. The deletion of rear fender skirts on the Sixty Special provoked yet more angst with tradition-minded Cadillac enthusiasts.

CHAPTER EIGHT, 1980–84

The most important resources drawn upon in the writing of this chapter include the author's interviews with John Middlebrook, William Hoglund and John Grettenberger, and the author's collection of General Motors- and Cadillac-related material.

1. The Imperial probably would have been even more appealing in a four-door configuration, and, around Chrysler, the failure of the Imperial launch was widely blamed on the decision to go with a coupe body style. This is probably scapegoating, though. The Seville and Continental were both four-door sedans, and neither of them set the sales charts on fire. The basic problem with the Imperial was that the brand name had long-since lost whatever small appeal it may once have had. By 1981, few people were interested in paying big bucks for a Chrysler product of any description.

2. This was another case where the lack of investment capital at Ford Motor Company saved the day for Lincoln. Lincoln did offer a turbo-diesel in its Mark VII and Continental lines in 1984, a fact which will no doubt come as a revelation to many readers (and should provide an indication of just how few were sold). In fact, Ford never built a passenger car diesel, but a deal had been struck with BMW to import a six-cylinder turbo-diesel specifically for Lincoln. Projections were for 8,000–10,000 units in 1984. Perhaps 3,800 were fitted, in all, before the program collapsed of its own dead weight. They were good diesels, but, thanks to problems with the Olds diesel, the diesel market had all-but evaporated by 1984. This collapse left General Motors with hundreds of thousands of angry owners, lots of very expensive and very useless plant capacity, and effectively ruined the diesel market for all manufacturers. The disaster tarnished even reputable builders such as Mercedes-Benz. Meanwhile, Ford was stuck with a lifetime supply of Lincoln replacement engines. Still, compared to General Motors, Ford—and Lincoln—got the better of the bargain by far.

3. In fact, it was quite easy to disarm the engine computer by simply snipping the wire that linked the computer to the transmission. By doing so, the engine was instantly reconverted to a straight V8—but few knew this little trick.

4. That the division knew the score on this point was revealed by an attempt on the part of Pontiac to upgrade its J-car 2000 with a leather interior in 1983 or 1984. Pontiac met with a furious intra-corporate attack from Cadillac and was forced to abandon its plans.

5. This meant that the Eldorado had its fifth basic engine in five years—not counting diesels.

6. A total of 52,082 V6-powered Cadillacs were built in the years 1980–82: 3,975 (1980); 30,444 (1981); and 17,663 (1982).

7. The first factory convertible to reappear from a Detroit manufacturer in the 1980s came about as a result of the exertions of one Lido A. Iacocca, formerly associated with Ford and then of Chrysler, who surprised the industry with a Chrysler LeBaron (and similar Dodge 400) convertible in 1982. By 1983, Chrysler had added a wood-paneled Town and Country version. Ford followed with the Mustang convertible in 1983. Buick then turned up with a limited edition 1983 Riviera convertible and Pontiac offered a few choptop J-car 2000s. All of these modern ragtops were factory authorized and/or commissioned conversions done on the outside, although Chrysler later brought its convertible production in-house.

8. Badge-engineering is the practice of applying more than one nameplate—or "badge," as the British say, which is where the term originated—to a given car line. In strict badge-engineering, little or nothing exists to differentiate the individual cars

in question except for their nameplates. This was certainly a major problem with General Motors J- and A-cars in the early 1980s.

9. Hoglund interview, author's collection.

10. Ibid.

11. Ibid. Fisher Body's margins were, indeed, huge. The Federal Trade Commission published an in-depth study of the auto industry in 1939 that explored the internal financial situation of General Motors in detail. In the eleven year period analyzed, 1927 to 1937, Fisher Body accounted for 28 percent of the combined net profit before taxes of the car divisions (Chevrolet, Chevrolet Trucks, Pontiac, Oldsmobile, Buick, Cadillac, and Fisher Body). In 1932, the only year in the post-Durant era in which General Motors posted a corporate loss prior to the 1980-82 recession, the car divisions posted a combined loss of $4.5 million. In contrast, Fisher Body's margins still enabled it to report a net profit of $5.2 million. Because of transfer pricing a component division such as Fisher Body, which did nearly all its business with other divisions, was bulletproof. Being a component division of General Motors prior to the 1984 reorganization was tantamount to having a license to print money.

12. Ibid.

13. Ibid.

14. Stempel interview, author's collection.

CHAPTER NINE, 1985–91

The most important resources drawn upon in the writing of this chapter include the author's interviews with Bob Stempel, John Middlebrook, William Hoglund and John Grettenberger, and the author's collection of General Motors- and Cadillac-related material.

1. In a curious about-face, Cadillac was back in the diesel business in 1985, perhaps under corporate pressure to make use of all the diesel production capacity previously noted. A V6 diesel was offered in the new front-drive models, while a reworked V8 version was listed for the Seville and Eldorado. A grand total of 995 V6s and 106 V8s were installed. Thus endeth the sorry story of the diesel at Cadillac (and at GM, as well).

2. It may have been. Another top designer at General Motors upon hearing of this conversation several months later, exclaimed: "Chuck said that?! He must have been pulling your leg!"

3. Known locally as Poletown, due to its historic ethnic make-up. The new facility was built, ironically, just down the street from the boarded-up remains of the old Packard factory.

4. Well, almost everybody. Cadillac's public relations department, which had a hard-won reputation for insufferable arrogance in this era, blamed the customers. Snapped the public relations director when asked why Cadillac was no longer viewed as the standard of the world: "You've got that backwards; it's the market that changed." Did it ever.

5. AutoWeek, November, 1986.

6. Hoglund interview, author's collection.

7. Ibid.

8. Hoglund interview, author's collection.

9. Ibid.

10. The upheaval at Cadillac public relations finally took place early in 1990. The new public relations director remarked to this writer in 1991, "I've spent the last year-and-a-half trying to rebuild relationships." In fairness, it should be noted that this writer had his share of problems with Cadillac public relations in this era—most journalists covering the "beat" did—although nothing unusual by prevailing standards. It should also be noted that John Grettenberger was consistently charming—even generous—in his personal dealings with the press corps, and always enjoyed a generally favorable reputation with that always-prickly group.

11. This writer had been trying for several years to obtain a rear-drive Brougham for the purpose of doing a magazine road test feature. Cadillac public relations resolutely refused to make one available, presumably on the theory that if unruly customers didn't read about the Brougham they wouldn't be uncooperative enough to want one. A Brougham was finally obtained from an unlikely source. Lincoln-Mercury had one they were using for comparative evaluation in the development of their forthcoming 1990 Town Car and, after some bemused consideration, made it available.

12. Grettenberger interview, author's collection.

CHAPTER TEN, 1992–2001

The most important resources drawn upon in the writing of this chapter include the author's interview with Bob Stempel, John Middlebrook, and John Grettenberger, and the author's collection of General Motors- and Cadillac-related material.

1. *Palm Springs Life*, November, 1989.
2. General Motors Corp. papers, author's collection.
3. General Motors Corp. papers, author's collection.
4. General Motors Corp. papers, author's collection.

CHAPTER ELEVEN, 2002–UP

The most important resources drawn upon in the writing of this chapter include the author's collection of General Motors- and Cadillac-related material.

1–14. General Motors Corp. papers, author's collection.

Bibliography

PRIMARY SOURCES

Books

Bennett, Harry. *We Never Called Him Henry*. New York, 1951.
Chrysler Corporation. Annual Reports, brochures and miscellaneous publications. Highland Park, Michigan.
Detroit Public Library, Automotive History Collection.
Ford Archives, Henry Ford Museum
Ford Motor Company. Annual Reports, brochures and miscellaneous publications. Detroit, Michigan.
General Motors Corporation. Annual Reports, brochures and miscellaneous publications. Detroit, Michigan.
Hudson Motor Car Company. Annual Reports, brochures and miscellaneous publications. Detroit, Michigan.
Packard Motor Car Company. Annual Reports, brochures and miscellaneous publications. Detroit, Michigan.
Pfau, Hugo. *The Custom Body Era*. New York, 1970.
Sloan, Alfred P. *Adventures of a White-Collar Man*. New York, 1941.
Sloan, Alfred P., Jr. *My Years With General Motors*. Garden City, New York, 1964.
Sorensen, Charles E. *My Forty Years With Ford*. New York, 1956.
Stout, Richard H. *Make 'Em Shout Hooray!* New York, 1988.
Studebaker Corporation (Delaware). Annual Reports, brochures and miscellaneous publications. South Bend, Indiana.
Studebaker-Packard Corporation. Annual Reports, brochures and miscellaneous publications. Detroit, Michigan, and South Bend, Indiana.
Studebaker-Packard Papers, George Arents Research Library, Syracuse University. Syracuse, New York.
Studebaker-Worthington Corporation. Annual Reports and miscellaneous publications. New York, New York.
Western Reserve Historical Society, Cleveland, Ohio.

Interviews

By the author with John Conde, Gary Cowger, Charles Jordan, Mark Gjovic, E. T. "Bob" Gregorie, John Grettenberger, Franklin Q. Hershey, William Hoglund, David Holls, Semon E. Knudsen, Holden Koto, Strother MacMinn, John Middlebrook, Sergio Pininfarina, Richard Stout, Richard Teague, and Rich Thomas.

Periodicals

Action Era Vehicle, Advertising Age, American Way, Argosy, Autocar (G.B.), *Auto Age, Automobile Quarterly, Automobile Show, Automobile, Automotive Industries, Automotive News, Automobile Topics, AutoWeek, Boston Globe, Business Week, Car Classics, Car Craft, Car & Driver, Car Life, CARS, Cars & Parts, Consumer Reports, Detroit News, Esquire, Forbes, Fortune, Handbook of Gasoline Automobiles, Horseless Age, Motor* (G.B.), *Hot Rod, Industrial Design, Mechanix Illustrated, Motor* (U.S.), *Motor Age, Motor Life, Motor Trend, Motor Trend Yearbook* (1955–61), *N.A.D.A. Used Car Guide* (various issues, 1934–67), *Newsweek, New York Times, Popular Mechanics, Popular Science, Road & Track, Scientific American, Special-Interest Autos, Sports Car Graphic, Time, True's Automobile Yearbook* (1953–60), *Wall Street Journal, Ward's,* and *Washington Post.*

SECONDARY SOURCES

Allen, Frederick Lewis. *The Big Change: America Transforms Itself, 1900–1950.* New York, 1952.

Barker, Ronald and Anthony Harding. *Automobile Design: Great Designers and Their Work.* Cambridge, Massachussetts, 1970.

Beasely, Norman and George W. Stark. *Made in Detroit.* New York, 1957.

Boyd, T. A. *Professional Amateur.* New York, 1957.

Brierly, Brooks T. *Auburn, Reo, Franklin and Pierce-Arrow versus Cadillac, Chrysler, Lincoln and Packard.* Coconut Grove, Florida, 1991.

Brinkley, David. *Washington Goes to War.* New York, 1988.

Bury, Martin H. *The Automobile Dealer.* Philadelphia, 1958.

Catton, Bruce. *The War Lords of Washington.* New York, 1948.

Chandler, Alfred D., Jr. *Giant Enterprise.* New York, 1964.

Cohn, David L. *Combustion On Wheels.* Boston, 1944.

Colins, Herbert Ridgeway. *Presidents On Wheels.* New York, 1971.

Conde, John. *American Motors Family Album.* Detroit, 1969.

Cornell Auto Publications. *Automobile Value Review.* Chicago, 1941.

Crabb, Richard. *Birth of a Giant.* New York, 1969.

Cravens, J. K. *Automobile Year Book and Buyer's Guide Illustrated.* Chicago, 1934.

Cravens, J. K. *Automobile Year Book and Buyer's Guide Illustrated.* Chicago, 1937.

Cray, Ed. *Chrome Colossus.* New York, 1980.

Drucker, Peter F. *Concept of the Corporation.* New York, 1946.

Drucker, Peter F. *The Practice of Management.* New York, 1954.

Editors of Automobile Quarterly. *The American Car Since 1775.* New York, 1971.

Georgano, G. N., ed. *The Complete Encyclopedia of Commercial Vehicles.* Osceola, Wisconsin, 1979.

Georgano, G. N., ed. *The Complete Encyclopedia of Motorcars: 1885 to the Present.* New York, 1973.

Gustin, Lawrence R. *Billy Durant, Creator of General Motors.* Grand Rapids, Michigan, 1973.

Heasley, Jerry. *The Production Figure Book for U.S. Cars.* Osceola, Wisconsin, 1977.

Hendry, Maurice. *Cadillac: The Standard of the World.* Princeton, New Jersey, 1973.

Herndon, Booton. *Ford.* New York, 1969.

Iacocca, Lido A. *Iacocca, An Autobiography.* New York, 1984.

Keats, John. *Insolent Chariots.* Philadelphia, 1958.

Kimes, Beverly R., ed. *Packard: A History of the Motorcar and the Company.* Princeton, New Jersey, 1978.

Kimes, Beverly Rae, and Henry Austin Clark, Jr. *Standard Catalog of American Cars 1805–1942.* Iola, Wisconsin, 1985.

Lacey, Robert. *Ford: The Men and the Machine.* New York, 1986.

Langworth, Richard M. *Studebaker, 1946–1966.* Osceola, Wisconsin, 1979.

Langworth, Richard M. *The Last Onslaught on Detroit.* Princeton, New Jersey, 1975.

Leland, Mrs. Wilfred C., and Mrs. Minnie Dubbs Milbrook. *Master of Precision.* Detroit, 1966.

Leslie, Stuart W. *Boss Kettering, Wizard of General Motors.* New York, 1983.

MacMinn, Strother, and Michael Lamm. *Detroit Style, Automotive Form 1925–1950.* Detroit, 1985.

Nesbitt, Dick. *50 Years of American Automobile Design.* Chicago, 1985.

Nevins, Allan, and Frank E. Hill. *Ford: Expansion and Challenge, 1915–1932.* New York, 1957.

Nevins, Allan, and Frank E. Hill. *Ford: Decline and Rebirth, 1933–1962.* New York, 1957.

Nevins, Allan, and Frank E. Hill. *Ford: The Times the Man and the Company.* New York, 1954.

Pound, Arthur. *The Turning Wheel: The Story of General Motors Through Twenty-Five Years, 1908–1933.* Garden City, New York, 1934

Rae, John B. *The American Automobile.* Chicago, 1965.

Riggs, L. Spencer. *Pace Cars of the Indy 500.* Ft. Lauderdale, Florida, 1989.

Sedgwick, Michael. *Cars of the 1930s.* Cambridge, Massachusetts, 1970.

Sedgwick, Michael. *Cars of the Thirties and Forties.* New York, 1979.

Sedgwick, Michael. *Cars of the 50s and 60s.* New York, 1983.

Turnquist, Robert E. *The Packard Story.* New York, 1965.

United States Government, Federal Trade Commission. *Report on Motor Vehicle Industry.* Washington, D.C., 1939.

Used Car Statistical Bureau. *Market Analysis Report.* Boston, 1941.

Ward, James A. *The Fall of the Packard Motor Car Company.* Stanford, California, 1995.

Weisberger, Bernard A. *The Dream Maker.* New York, 1979.

Wilkie, David J. and the editors of Esquire. *American Autos and Their Makers.* New York, 1963.

Young, Clarence H., and William A. Quinn. *Foundation for Living.* New York, 1963.

Index

Printed and bound by CPI Group (UK) Ltd, Croydon, CR0 4YY

16/04/2025

14658407-0001